THE MEN,
THE MEANING,
THE MESSAGE
OF THE NEW TESTAMENT BOOKS

A Series of New Testament Studies

By
WILLIAM BARCLAY

THE WESTMINSTER PRESS: PHILADELPHIA

Library of Congress Cataloging in Publication

Barclay, William, lecturer in the University of Glasgow.
    The men, the meaning, the message of the New Testament books.

    First published in 1976 under title: The men, the
meaning, the message of the books.
    Includes bibliographies.
    1. Bible. N.T. — Introductions. I. Title.
BS2330.2.B32 1978   225.6   77-22184
ISBN 0-664-24188-3

Published in Great Britain under the title
The Men, The Meaning, The Message of the Books

Published by The Westminster Press ®
Philadelphia, Pennsylvania

PRINTED IN THE UNITED STATES OF AMERICA
9 8 7 6 5 4 3

CONTENTS

FOREWORD

The chapters of this book appeared first as a series of monthly articles in *Life and Work*, the magazine of the Church of Scotland. The idea was to take a quick but comprehensive view of the whole New Testament. It may well be that there are occasions when we do well to depart from the idea of the New Testament as a repository of texts, and stand back to look at it as a whole. The origin of these chapters explains much of their character. Since they were magazine articles, the space available for them was limited, and therefore there was a strict restraint on the number of things which could be said. The plan was to find one basic idea which is the main theme of each book, so that the book could be read around that idea. This collection then has no value in itself, unless it sends its readers to read again, or to read for the first time, the New Testament itself.

My warmest thanks are due to Mr Robert Kernohan, the Editor of *Life and Work*, for allowing me in the first place to write the articles, and in the second place to publish them in this form; and I am very much indebted to the editorial staff of the Saint Andrew Press for undertaking, and saving me from, the time-consuming task of proof correction.

It is my hope and my prayer that these ephemeral chapters will send the reader to the eternal book, about which they are written.

WILLIAM BARCLAY.

INTRODUCTION

Six honest serving-men

In his book *How to read the Bible* F. C. Grant tells of an experience which happened to a friend of his. His friend had been giving an address to a group of people on how to read the Bible. No sooner had he finished than a young woman rose and said: 'You don't need someone to tell you how to read the Bible. Open it anywhere, read three verses, make your mind a blank, and the Holy Spirit will do the rest!' For a point of view like that there is no such thing as Bible *study*.

Benjamin E. Mays, the great negro educator, in his book *Born to Rebel*, tells how in his young days among many of the negroes there was an actual prejudice against education. He himself in the end had to defy his own father to get his education. The attitude was that 'God *called* men to preach, and when he called them, he would tell them what to say!' Education, study, were superfluous.

No one is going to deny that the simplest and the most unlettered person, with no aids to study at all, can find the word of God in the Bible, and can discover there strength for life, comfort for sorrow, and guidance for action. But it is also true that the more we bring to the Bible, the more we will get from the Bible.

There is more than one level at which we may listen to anything. Take the case of music. We may listen to a great symphony simply as a marvellous river of sound. That is the

1

simplest way of listening. We may study the programme notes, and we may see the structure of the music. We may see how the themes enter and are developed and interwoven by the composer. That brings something more to the study of the music. We may, before we listen, find out something about the life and experience of the composer, so that we know something of the situation out of which the music was born. That clearly will make the music more meaningful yet.

Take the case of Beethoven's Ninth Symphony. We may listen to it, knowing no more than that this is sound and melody which thrills the ear and speaks to the heart. We may study the programme notes, and we can hear the pattern of the music developing, as we listen for the entry of each instrument and the development of each theme. Before we come to the performance, we can learn something of the life of Beethoven, and we can become aware that it was out of the prison of total deafness that Beethoven wrote that symphony, and that he never heard it except in his mind. To know *that* will make listening to that symphony one of the most moving experiences that music can bring.

The Bible is like this. Of course, the simplest person can open it and read it. But the more we know about the Bible, the more thrilling and fascinating this book becomes.

In one of his poems Kipling writes:

> 'I keep six honest serving-men
> (They taught me all I knew);
> Their names are What and Why and When
> And How and Where and Who.'

In the opening lines of his *Introduction to First Peter*, F. J. A. Hort writes: 'To understand a book rightly, we want to know who wrote it, for what readers it was written, for what purposes, and under what circumstances.' In other words, we need to call in Kipling's six honest serving-men when we want really and fully to study any book, and to study the Bible.

Let us look at some of the questions, even if in our space we cannot look at them all.

It matters very much *who* says a thing. I remember once being at a concert at which a baritone came on and sang Henley's *Invictus*.

> 'Out of the night which covers me,
> Black as the pit from pole to pole,
> I thank whatever gods there be
> For my unconquerable soul.'

As the man turned to leave the platform after singing, I suddenly saw what I had not noticed when he came on. *He was blind.* It makes a difference when a blind man can sing that. We read in Romans (8: 28): 'We know that in everything God works for good'. This would not be a very impressive saying from one on whom the cold wind had never been allowed to blow. But the man who said it was the man who had, not the thorn, but the stake (*skolops*) turning and twisting in his flesh and making life an agony (2 Corinthians 12: 7). When a man can never be free of pain, and yet affirm that in his experience God does all things well—this means something.

It matters very much *when* a thing is said. It was 'in the year that King Uzziah died' that Isaiah had his vision—and that was a year of tragedy (Isaiah 6: 1). Uzziah or Azariah had been one of the great and good kings. But in one reckless moment he had insisted on himself burning incense in the temple, and then and there he had become a leper. That was the year in which the splendour of the king had finished up in a lazar house (2 Kings 15: 1-5; 2 Chronicles 26: 16-21). As George Adam Smith puts it: 'The king sank into a leper's grave, but before Isaiah's vision the divine majesty arose in all its loftiness.' To have the vision of God in a sunlit time would no doubt be great, but to have vision of God when life is shot through with sheer tragedy is greater yet—and that is what Isaiah had.

It matters very much *where* a thing is said. One of the great things that Paul said is in the letter to the Corinthians 'Neither the immoral, nor adulterers, nor idolaters, nor homosexuals, nor thieves, nor greedy, nor drunkards, nor revilers, nor robbers, will inherit the kingdom of God. *And such were some of you*' (1 Corinthians 6: 9, 10).

Corinth was the city with the temple of Aphrodite which had a thousand priestesses who were sacred prostitutes, and who came down to the city streets to ply their trade each evening, so that the Greeks had a saying, 'It is not everyone who can afford a journey to Corinth.' It was commonly said that no Corinthian was ever introduced in a play on the stage other than blind drunk. There was a Greek verb *korinthiazesthai*, derived from the name Corinth, which means to indulge in drunken revelry.

The letter begins with an address to 'the church of God which is at Corinth' (1 Corinthians 1: 2). The church of God which is at *Corinth*—Bengel's comment is, 'a huge and happy paradox'. It was not in some respectable part of suburbia that the grace of God operated mightily—it was at *Corinth*.

It can often happen that the simple placing of an incident in its context sheds a new light on it. Take the case of the incident in which James and John, or their mother, seek to gain from Jesus a guarantee of the chief places when he comes into his kingdom. (Matthew 20: 20, 21; Mark 10: 35-37). This is often quoted as an example of the earthly ambition of the disciples, and of their inability to think except in terms of an earthly kingdom. Maybe it is. But it is something more. It is one of the greatest examples of faith in all the gospel story.

Jesus was on his way to Jerusalem; it was clear that there was going to be a head-on clash with the Jewish authorities. He had told them again and again of the cross which loomed ahead; but the James and John who made this request could not think of Jesus in any other terms than in terms of ultimate triumph. This may have been a request of ambition, but it was also the request of men whose faith in Jesus was unshaken, even when the storm clouds were gathering.

No one is going to deny that anyone can read the Bible. But not only to read it but also to study it will make it shine with a new light. It makes all the difference *who* said a thing; it makes all the difference *when* it was said; it makes all the difference *where* it was said.

In this book we shall be studying the New Testament together. The method which I propose to use is this. I think that it is possible to find in each book of the New Testament one basic, dominant idea. I think that it is possible in each book to find one special thing which that book was written to say.

Of course, there is much more than one idea even in the shortest and the simplest books; but at the heart of each book there is one idea which is the moving cause of the whole matter. So I hope that in the pages that follow we will pass the New Testament books in review before us and will find the one great thing which each has to say, and that then we will read each book in the light of its dominating idea.

We shall begin by looking at the Gospel Matthew wrote, and we shall see that it comes rightly at the beginning of the New Testament, because it is the Gospel which binds the Testaments together.

1 · The bridge between

The Gospel of Matthew

The New Testament books do not appear in the same order in all the ancient manuscripts. For instance, in *Codex Bezae*, which is one of the most famous manuscripts, the Gospels appear in the order Matthew, John, Luke, Mark.

But one thing remains constant; in every manuscript of the New Testament Matthew comes first. That is not because Matthew was the first book to be written. Some of Paul's letters were written forty years before Matthew was written. Matthew was not even the first of the Gospels to be written; Mark is the earliest gospel, written perhaps twenty-five years before Matthew was written. Yet Matthew comes first, and comes first always. And this is so because Matthew is the bridge between the Old and the New Testaments.

Of all the books of the New Testament, Matthew is the book which draws the two Testaments together. Why is this so? Matthew sees Jesus as the fulfilment of the hopes and the dreams of the Jewish nation, and of the fulfilment of the promises of God to his people.

In Matthew, Jesus is called Son of David oftener than in all the other Gospels put together (Matthew 1: 1; 9: 27; 12: 23; 15: 22; 20: 30, 31; 21: 9, 15). The only place in Mark and Luke where Jesus is definitely called Son of David is in the incident of the blind man (Mark 10: 47, 48; Luke 18: 38, 39), and in John he is never definitely called Son of David at all.

To see just how characteristic of Matthew this is, all we have to do is to read the story of Jesus' entry into Jerusalem in the four Gospels (Matthew 21: 1-9; Mark 11: 1-10; Luke 19: 28-38; John 12: 12-19), where we can see that only in Matthew's version of the story is Jesus hailed as Son of David.

Quite early in the history of the Church the four living creatures of Revelation 4: 7 were taken to be the emblems of the four Gospels. The allocation of the symbols varies—they can often be seen in stained-glass windows.

In Irenaeus, the man stands for Matthew; the eagle for Mark; the ox for Luke; the lion for John. In Victorinus, the man stands for Matthew; the lion for Mark; the ox for Luke; and the eagle for John. But the allocation which became most common, and which was to become the standard allocation was that of Augustine—the lion for Matthew; the man for Mark; the ox for Luke; the eagle for John.

The symbolism is that Mark gives us the most human picture of Jesus and may fitly be represented by the man. Luke gives us the picture of Jesus as the sacrifice for the sins of the whole world, and may fitly be represented by the ox, the animal of sacrifice. The eagle flies higher than any other bird, and is said to be the only living creature which can look straight into the sun and not be dazzled, and therefore fitly stands for John, who is the greatest thinker of all. The lion is the Lion of Judah, and that is the title of the Messiah, and it is as the Messiah, the Lion of Judah, the Son of David, that Matthew sees Jesus.

Clearly, this is something for Jews. To call Jesus 'Son of David' to a Greek would mean nothing, for he would have no idea who David was, or what David's Son was supposed to be. Matthew was a Jew speaking to Jews. His book fitly joins the Old Testament to the New.

So, then, Matthew is presenting Jesus to the Jews as the Messiah whom they had so long expected, and whom they had so tragically failed to recognise when he came. If Matthew ever hoped to persuade the Jews to accept Jesus as Messiah, he could only do so in one way—by demonstrating that Jesus fulfilled in himself the prophecies that the prophets had made.

This is why there runs through the whole of Matthew one characteristic phrase. We meet it in the first chapter and we go on meeting it all through the book—'All this took place to fulfil what the Lord had spoken by the prophet' (Matthew 1: 22; 2: 15, 17, 23; 4: 14; 8: 17; 12: 17; 13:35; 21: 4; 26: 56; 27: 9).

It is quite true that, sometimes, Matthew claims to be using prophecy in a way in which we cannot use it now. In 2: 15 he takes the sentence, 'Out of Egypt have I called my son' as a prophecy of the journey and the return of Joseph and Mary and Jesus into and from Egypt. It is a quotation of Hosea 11: 1, which reads:

> 'When Israel was a child, I loved him,
> And out of Egypt I called my son.
> The more I called them,
> the more they went from me;
> They kept sacrificing to the Baals,
> and burning incense to idols.'

In Hosea the sentence is a statement of past history, a statement that God delivered Israel from slavery in Egypt, and that Israel was ungrateful for the deliverance and disobedient to the God who had rescued them. Simply because the words *Egypt, call* and *son* were there, Matthew had annexed this as a prophecy of something with which it had nothing to do.

True, we cannot argue like that. But that is not the point. This is exactly the way in which a Jewish Rabbi would argue, and this is an argument which would be quite convincing to a Jew. This was not written to convince a twentieth century

Scotsman; it was written to convince a first century Jew. And this it would do.

So, then, Matthew was out to show Jesus as the fulfilment of the hopes and dreams of the Jewish nation, and the way in which he did it was to argue that in Jesus the prophecies were fulfilled. But there is more to Matthew than that. If this was all that Matthew had to offer, then he would be offering a Jewish Jesus.

But James Moffatt (*Introduction to the Literature of the New Testament*, p. 244) distinguishes three ways in which Jesus goes far beyond Judaism as Matthew sees it.

(a) Right at the beginning (Matthew 1: 21) it is said: 'You shall call his name Jesus, for he will save his people from their sins.' In the old Judaism a man was going to be saved because he was a Jew; now a man is going to be saved, not because he is a Jew, but because he belongs in faith to Jesus Christ. Salvation has become the product not of nationality but of faith. This is precisely what the saying means; that the Church is the new Israel, the Israel of God (Galatians 6: 16). All the promises that once belonged to the nation of Israel now belong to those whose faith is in Christ.

(b) The claim of Jesus to the critical Pharisees is: 'I tell you something greater than the temple is here' (Matthew 12: 6). To the Jew there was nothing in the world more sacred than the Temple; there was no place in the world where a man was nearer God than in the Temple. But this is transcended in Jesus Christ. It is not in the Temple but in him that God is nearest of all.

(c) In the Sermon on the Mount it is the very essence that the new teaching of Jesus Christ transcends the old teaching of the Law. 'You have heard that it has been said, but *I* tell you . . .' (Matthew 5: 17, 21, 27, 31, 33, 38, 43). To the Jew the Law was supremely the voice of God; but in Jesus Christ the voice of God spoke with an authority that surpassed even that of the Law.

To Matthew, Jesus is not simply the fulfilment of Judaism; he is that which goes beyond all that Judaism ever dreamed of. In him the salvation of God comes not to a nation but to the world. In him the presence of God is nearer than it had been in the most sacred place known to the Jews. In him the voice of God speaks with an authority which surpassed even the authority of the Law. Here is God in a way that not even the Old Testament ever knew.

Matthew comes at the beginning of the New Testament because he does two things. He ties the New Testament firmly to the Old Testament. Bruce Metzger in his *Introduction to the Apocrypha* (p. 151) writes: 'It must be said at the outset that the indispensable aid for a correct understanding of the New Testament is the Old Testament. All the New Testament writers presuppose the Old Testament foundation, the Hebrew history and covenant. The Church is so much the heir of the Old Testament that it calls itself the Israel of God.'

Matthew is the proof that we can never jettison or discard the Old Testament, for out of the Old the New was born. But Matthew does more than that. Jesus is not simply the fulfilment of Jewish hopes. In him God did something utterly and completely new. Matthew is the bridge between, the Gospel in which uniquely the old and the new join hands.

Questions for discussion

1. Matthew makes Jesus 'the fulfilment of the hopes and dreams of the Jewish nation'. But did Jesus not also disappoint their hopes? In what ways does Jesus attract and in what ways does he repel the loyalty of ordinary folk?

2. The symbols of eagle, lion, etc. appear in stained-glass. Is there anything to be said for using such symbols in Churches except that they can look colourful?

3. Matthew speaks of Jesus as Messiah. It meant something to the Jews no doubt. What does it mean to you?

4. 'The promises that once belonged to . . . Israel now belong to those whose faith is in Christ.' From your knowledge of the Old Testament could you list some of those promises?

5. The Jews had to be rebuked for idolising the Temple. Is it possible that, even with us, people may put their loyalty to the Temple—i.e. their Church—before their obedience to Christ?

Further reading
Commentaries by William Barclay (*Daily Study Bible*), F. V. Filson (*A. and C. Black*), R. V. G. Tasker (*Tyndale*).

2 · The Man of Galilee

The Gospel of Mark

Most scholars would agree that there are two things about Mark's Gospel which are of supreme importance. First, it is very widely agreed that Mark was the first of the Gospels to be written, and that it was the basis of both Matthew and Luke. There are 661 verses in Mark. Of these 661 verses, Matthew reproduces 606 and Luke reproduces 320. Of Mark's 661 verses there are only 31 which do not appear somewhere in Matthew or Luke. All the indications are that Mark was the first Gospel to be written and that Matthew and Luke used him as the basis of their Gospels.

There is one other significant fact. Matthew and Luke in general follow Mark's order of events. Occasionally both Matthew and Luke may vary the order, but, as far as the order of the events of Jesus' life goes, Matthew and Luke never together vary from Mark; one of them always agrees with him, and most often both.

Second, a man called Papias was Bishop of Hierapolis in South Phrygia in the first half of the second century. He was a great collector of information about the Gospels, and he tells us that Mark's Gospel is in fact the preaching material of Peter. He says that Mark was Peter's 'interpreter', and that he accurately set down the things that Peter used to preach about Jesus.

If this is so, we have in Mark what is next door to an

eye-witness account of the life of Jesus. There are in Mark
certain vivid details which read very much as if they were the
memories of someone who was there. In the story of the storm
at sea only Mark says that Jesus was asleep on a cushion in the
stern of the boat (4: 37). Only Mark tells us that, when Jesus
saw the rich young ruler, he loved him (10: 21). When Mark is
telling the stories of Jesus and the children, only he says that
Jesus took the little ones up in the crook of his arm (9: 36;
10: 16). When we read Mark, we should always be on the watch
for the little vivid extra things which only he has.

There is still another thing about Mark in which we seem to
hear again the voice of Jesus. Mark has a habit, shared by none
of the other Gospel writers, of giving Jesus' words in the
original Aramaic.

Only Mark tells us that Jesus said to the little girl, 'Talitha
cumi' (5: 41). Only Mark tells us that Jesus said to the deaf
man, 'Ephphatha', that his ears might be opened (7: 34). Only
Mark shows us Jesus in the Garden calling God 'Abba', the
word by which a little Jewish child called his father in the circle
of the home (14: 36). It is likely that, when Peter told these
stories, he heard again the voice of his Lord, and slipped into
his native Aramaic, the Aramaic which Jesus had spoken.

There is an almost childlike simplicity in the way in which
Mark tells his stories. This comes out specially in three ways.

(a) One of Mark's ways we do not see in the English
translation, because the English translation has 'improved'
Mark. Mark is very fond of the historic present. This is to say
he writes his narrative in the present tense—'She says to me,
and I says to her', and so on, just as simple people tell a story.
In the Greek there are 151 of these 'historic presents' in Mark.

(b) Mark is astonishingly fond of the word 'and'; he tells a
story by just going on adding 'and . . . and . . . and'. In the
Greek of chapter 3, 29 out of the 35 verses begin with 'and'.

(c) Mark is very fond of the word 'immediately'. It occurs 41 times in his Gospel. In the first chapter alone it occurs 10 times (1: 10, 12, 18, 20, 21, 23, 28, 29, 30, 42). It is sometimes said that a story marches; but Mark's story gallops, with event following event with breathless rapidity.

We have said that Mark came first; and we have said that Mark had a simple mind. This quite often resulted in him putting things in a way that the later Gospels 'corrected'. We take three examples of this.

In the story of the rejection of Jesus at Nazareth, Mark says (6: 5): 'And he could do no mighty work there, except that he laid his hands upon a few sick people and healed them.' When Matthew comes to tell this story (13: 58) he is unwilling to say that there was something Jesus *could not do*, that Jesus was unable to do. So he changes it very slightly but very significantly: 'And he did not do many mighty works there, because of their unbelief.' Mark says that Jesus *could* not do it, Matthew that he *did* not do it.

In the story of the rich young ruler, the young man says to Jesus, as Mark tells the story, 'Good Teacher, what must I do to inherit eternal life?' Jesus answers: 'Why do you call me good? No one is good but God alone' (10: 17, 18). Matthew does not like this and he alters Jesus' return question to: 'Why do you ask me about what is good? One there is who is good' (19: 16, 17). Mark is too simple to be theologically worried by Jesus refusing the title 'good'. Matthew is worried and changes it.

In the story of the ambition of James and John, in Mark the request for the chief places is made by James and John themselves (10: 17-22). In Matthew's version of the story the request is made by their mother (20: 20-28). And thus Matthew preserves the two disciples from the charge of selfish ambition.

This is the whole beauty of Mark. J. H. Ropes speaks of

Mark's 'incomparable touch of reality'. A. B. Bruce said: 'In Mark we get nearest to the true human personality of Jesus in all its originality and power. . . . One who desires to see the Jesus of history truly should con well the pages of Mark first.'

We have said that Mark may well be dependent on the preaching of Peter. There could be, in one place, more than that. Mark's family was at the very centre of the Church. From Acts it becomes clear that the house of Mark's mother was the centre of the Church, for that is where Peter went when he escaped from prison (Acts 12: 12).

Now it is not at all impossible that it was in this house belonging to Mark's mother that the Last Supper was eaten. This may well be the explanation of one very odd verse in Mark. Mark 14: 51, 52 tells of the young man in the linen cloth who escaped naked from the arrest of Jesus. Why on earth is that strange irrelevant verse put into the Gospel? Maybe because the young man was Mark, in whose home the Supper had been, and who had fled out into the night. This could be Mark's signature on his Gospel.

There is one thing above all that Mark has done; once and for all he established the pattern of the life of Jesus. That pattern was a drama in four acts. In the first act we see the preparation of Jesus (1: 1-20) in his baptism, his temptations and the call of his disciples. In the second act there comes the long conflict (1: 21-13: 37). Then there comes the bitter tragedy of the passion and the Cross (14: 1-15: 47). And finally there comes the triumph of the Resurrection (16). The four act drama—preparation, conflict, tragedy, triumph—this we owe to the shaping of Mark.

We note one last thing. The text of Mark's Gospel properly finishes at 16: 8, as the Revised Standard Version and the New English Bible both show. Mark 16: 9-19 is not part of the original Gospel. Now it is hardly likely that the Gospel originally ended at 16: 8, for that would be a very abrupt ending. It may well be that, when Matthew and Luke had annexed Mark and woven him into their Gospels, Mark was for a time totally neglected, so neglected that in the end the last section of the only surviving copy was missing.

We ought to be thankful that this the most vivid of the Gospels was preserved, although it was so nearly lost. I have no no doubt at all that it is with Mark we should begin the reading of the New Testament, for here we are nearest of all to the historic Jesus. Sit down and read the whole Gospel at one sitting, and see again the panorama of the four acts of the life of Christ.

Questions for discussion

1. In thinking about Jesus, are we sometimes in more danger of losing sight of his humanity than forgetting his divinity?

2. What passages in Mark help us to keep the balance between Jesus' divinity and humanity?

3. In Mark, Peter is hardly ever mentioned except in a bad light. How much may this have to do with the fact that Peter's authority is behind Mark's Gospel? Does he wish us to see how Jesus loved and trusted Peter even after he had let Jesus down?

4. Do you agree that we ought more often to read the Gospels, especially Mark, right through at a sitting?

Further reading

Commentaries by William Barclay (*Daily Study Bible*), R. A. Cole (*Tyndale*), A. M. Hunter (*Torch*), D. E. Nineham (*Pelican*), A. E. J. Rawlinson (*Westminster*).

3 · The friend of the friendless

The Gospel of Luke

If ever I had to choose to keep one book of the New Testament, and one book only, the book I would choose would be Luke's Gospel, for in it I believe that we have Jesus at his most beautiful and the Gospel at its widest.

In the printed Revised Standard Version of the New Testament there are 552 pages. Luke's Gospel takes up 78 pages, and Acts, the other book which Luke wrote, takes up 71 pages; that is, 149 pages in all. This means that Luke wrote more than a quarter, 27% of the New Testament. Paul's letters take up only 121 pages, so Luke wrote even more of the New Testament than Paul did.

Strangely enough, we know very little about the man who was the largest contributor to the New Testament. From Colossians 4: 10-14 we know that Luke was a doctor and we can deduce that he was a Gentile. In Colossians 4: 11 Paul finishes listing the Jewish friends who were with him, so we can conclude that the others he mentions, among whom is Luke, were Gentiles. We know that Paul reckoned Luke as one of his fellow-workers (Philemon 24). And we know that, when everyone else had left Paul, Luke the faithful was still with him in prison in Rome.

In later days men believed that Luke stood to Paul in the same relation as Mark stood to Peter, and that, just as in his book Mark has given us the Gospel which Peter preached, so in his Gospel Luke has given us the Gospel that Paul preached. 'Luke the follower of Paul,' writes Irenaeus, 'recorded in a book the Gospel that was preached by him' (Irenaeus, *Against Heresies* 3: 1).

It is interesting to remember, as we read him, that Luke is the only writer in the New Testament who was not a Jew, and that more than a quarter of the New Testament was written by him. What then can we say of Luke and his writings?

1. First of all, we can say that Luke is the scholar of the New Testament. Luke 1: 1-4 is the best Greek in the New Testament. Further, that brief Prologue is exactly the same kind of thing that professional Greek historians used to begin their books. 'Luke', writes Jerome in his *Letter of Damasus*, 'was the most learned in the Greek language of all the evangelists.'

Further, it is quite clear that Luke's Gospel is a work of the most careful investigation and research. Luke had not himself known and seen Jesus, but he had carefully examined all the evidence and had weighed up all that he could find that had been written about Jesus, and then he wrote his Gospel. This is what he claims and tells us in his Prologue (Luke 1: 1-4).

This is interesting, because it means that inspiration and investigation and research can, and often must, go hand in hand. Sometimes we tend to think of an inspired writer writing, as it were, to the dictation of the Holy Spirit. But inspiration came to Luke as he pored over his books and examined and sifted his evidence and wrote with all the toil and research which an historian must bring to his task. When man's toil and God's Spirit unite, then the result is greatness.

2. But Luke was more than a scholar; Luke was a man. And it may be that we can read behind his narrative one of the greatest examples of sheer loyalty in the history of the Church. When, in Acts, Luke tells of Paul's last journey to Rome, he

tells it in the first person. 'We put to sea,' he says (Acts 27: 1, 2).

On that last journey Luke and Aristarchus were with Paul. It was the law that, when a prisoner set out to be tried before the Emperor, he might take with him two personal servants or slaves. And it may well have been that Luke and Aristarchus enrolled themselves as Paul's slaves, so as not to be separated from him in the closing act of his life. Then, and to the very end, Luke was with Paul (2 Timothy 4: 11). Luke was greater than a scholar; he was a man whose loyalty remained unshakeable to the end.

3. But Luke's scholarship was put to the most practical purposes. Luke was an apologist for Christianity and a defender of the faith. He addressed his Gospel and Acts, which are two volumes of the one book, to, as the RSV has it, 'most excellent Theophilus'. The word which is so translated is the honorific title commonly given to a high government official, and the NEB correctly renders it, 'Your excellency'.

Luke was writing in the days, between A.D. 80 and 90, when Christianity was beginning to be under attack, when the charges and the threats and the slanders were flying around, and it is highly probable that Luke wrote to Theophilus, the high official of the Roman government, to give him an account of the life of Jesus and of the Church, which would prove to him that Christianity was no evil thing, but the way of truth and life. It is significant that, when Luke wished to defend the Christian faith, he did not argue about it; he simply told the story of it.

It is just possible that the usual translation of Luke 1: 4 needs to be altered. The usual translation is that Luke's aim is to tell Theophilus the truth about the things of which he has been *informed*. It may well be that here the correct translation is not *informed* but *misinformed*, and that Luke writes to tell Theophilus the true facts about Jesus and about Christianity.

4. Luke is above all the man of compassion. His is the universal Gospel; his is the Gospel which shows, more than any other, Jesus as the friend of the friendless. All the Gospel writers begin by quoting Isaiah 40: 3. Only Luke continues the passage to include the saying: 'All flesh shall see the salvation of God' (Matthew 3: 3; Mark 1: 2, 3; John 1: 23; Luke 3: 4-6).

Again and again Luke shows the hated Samaritans in a good light (Luke 9: 51-56; 10: 30-37; 17: 11-19). From the very beginning Simeon sees in the infant Jesus 'a light for revelation to the Gentiles' (Luke 2: 32). It is the widow of Zarephath and Naaman the Syrian who are quoted as examples of faith (Luke 4: 25-27). It is the Gentile centurion who is the example of faith (Luke 7: 1-10).

Luke loves the poor (Luke 6: 20, 21, 24, 25; 14: 12-24; 16: 19-31). He loves to show Jesus in the company of those with whom no respectable Jew would have had anything to do: with the woman who was a sinner (Luke 7: 36-50); with Zacchaeus (19: 2-10); telling the story of the penitent tax-gatherer (18: 9-14); telling the stories of how much God loves to find the folk who have gone lost (Luke 15); promising the glory to a dying thief on a criminal's cross (Luke 23: 39-43).

In Palestine in the time of Jesus a woman was merely a thing with no legal rights whatsoever, with no education and no part in public life. But Luke's Gospel again and again draws loving portraits of the women who came into contact with Jesus: Elizabeth (Luke 1: 5, 24, 25, 57, 58); Anna the prophetess (Luke 2: 36-38); the widow of Nain (Luke 7: 11-17); the woman in Simon's house (Luke 7: 36-50); Mary Magdalene, out of whom he cast seven devils; Susanna; Joanna, the wife of Chuza, Herod's steward, and therefore a member of high society (Luke 8: 2); Martha and Mary (Luke 10: 38-41); the weeping daughters of Jerusalem (Luke 23: 27-31). Any good doctor is a man of compassion, and so was Luke.

5. We have left the most important of all Luke's characteristics to the end. *Luke was the first church historian.* Matthew and Mark thought in terms of an immediate Second Coming; Luke thought in terms of the Church. Matthew and Mark saw Jesus as the immediate end of history; Luke saw him as the midpoint of history. It is only Luke who goes beyond the Resurrection and writes the history of the Church in Acts.

Let us take two passages and see how the three Gospel-writers relate them. First, the saying of Jesus immediately after Caesarea Philippi and before the Transfiguration.

Matthew (16: 28) has it: 'Truly, I say to you, there are some standing here who will not taste death before they see the Son of Man coming in his kingdom.' Here is an unmistakable reference to the Second Coming. Mark (9: 1) has it: 'Truly, I say to you there are some standing here who will not taste death before they see the kingdom of God come with power.' Luke (9: 27): 'But I tell you truly, there are some standing here who will not taste death before they see the kingdom of God.' Mark and Luke substitute the spread of the kingdom for the Second Coming of Christ.

Second, the answer of Jesus to the high priest at his trial, when the high priest demanded to know whether or not he was the Messiah. Matthew (26: 64) has it: 'You have said so. But I tell you, hereafter you will see the Son of man seated at the right hand of Power, and coming on the clouds of heaven!' Mark (14: 62) has: 'I am; and you will see the Son of Man sitting at the right hand of power, and coming with the clouds of heaven.' Matthew and Mark give Jesus' answer unmistakably in terms of the Second Coming in the very near future. Luke (22: 67-69) has: 'If I tell you, you will not believe; and if I ask you, you will not answer. But from now on the Son of Man shall be seated at the right hand of the power of God. Luke has removed altogether the idea of the immediate Second Coming.

Here is the tremendous importance of Luke. The earlier Gospels thought of the end of time as about to come immediately. Luke thought of the age of the Church, in which not the end of time but the kingdom of God was to come. Luke is the discoverer of *Church* history. To the others Jesus was the end of history; to Luke Jesus was the beginning of salvation history. Luke is, as it were, the historian who discovered the place of the Church in the plan of God, and who thought not so much of the Second Coming of Jesus as of the coming of the Kingdom.

Luke thought of the life and death and Resurrection of Jesus not as the end but as the beginning of history. For Luke, Jesus Christ within the Church goes on being the friend of the friendless and the Saviour of the world.

Questions for discussion

1. Luke shows Jesus as the friend of the friendless. How can the Church carry on the work of being the friend of the friendless today?

2. What would you say to a preacher who says: 'I never prepare my sermons. I just get up and say what the Holy Spirit tells me to say'?

3. What does it mean to be loyal to Jesus today?

4. We have seen that the different Gospel writers report the sayings of Jesus in different ways. Does this trouble you? Or, do you see in this an instance of the work of the Holy Spirit in always leading men to see more clearly the meaning of what Jesus was saying?

Further reading
Commentaries by William Barclay (*Daily Study Bible*), G. B. Caird (*Pelican*), A. R. C. Leaney (*A. and C. Black*), W. Manson (*Moffatt*).

4 · The mind of God in human form

The Gospel of John

One has only to read through the Fourth Gospel to see that it is the Gospel which is different. For many it marks the peak of New Testament theology and revelation. Luther called it 'chiefest of the Gospels, unique, tender and true'. Jerome said that the man who wrote the Fourth Gospel was 'saturated with revelation'.

Sybil Thorndike tells how Gilbert Murray, the great Greek scholar, told her, when she began to study Greek, to read John's Gospel. 'It is bad Greek,' he said, 'but it will open a door for you.' And Sybil Thorndike says: 'And what a door it has opened!'

It is not for nothing that the common symbol of John's Gospel is the eagle, for the eagle flies higher than any other bird, and the eagle is said to be the only living creature which can look straight into the sun, and not be dazzled. The John of the Fourth Gospel is the eagle of New Testament thought. That this is true no one will deny, but nonetheless the Fourth Gospel has been a storm centre of problems. There have always been arguments about the authorship of the Fourth Gospel.

Hippolytus of Rome, who flourished round about A.D. 200, wrote a book entitled *In Defence of the Gospel according to St John and the Revelation*. No one defends what is not attacked, and in those early days the Fourth Gospel was attacked as a modernist work, which had strayed from the simplicities of the real Gospel story.

In the Gospel itself there is what we might call a double citation. A witness is cited, and he is said to have been an eye-witness of the events of the Cross (John 19: 35). Then further, in the Gospel there appears a character called the Beloved Disciple. This Beloved Disciple was reclining on Jesus' right at the Last Supper (John 13: 23). (They reclined on couches to eat in those days, leaning on the left elbow, with the feet stretched out behind, and the right hand free to use. Therefore, the Beloved Disciple was on Jesus' right, with his head on Jesus' shoulder.) The Beloved Disciple is at the Cross (John 19: 26). He is at the empty tomb (John 20: 2). He is at the lakeside (John 21: 7), and he is finally named as the author or compiler of the Gospel (John 21: 20-24). The strange thing is that John is not mentioned in the Fourth Gospel at all, from beginning to end. (John the Baptist is, but not John the Apostle.)

Let us add the further things we know. There is no doubt that tradition always ascribes the Fourth Gospel to John the Apostle, but in tradition there is regularly the statement that the Fourth Gospel is a communal production. Clement of Alexandria says that John wrote 'urged by his companions' (Eusebius, *The Ecclesiastical History* 6.14.5).

Jerome in his prologue to the Fourth Gospel says that John wrote urged by all the bishops of Asia Minor and by the delegates of the Churches. And in his book entitled *Illustrious Men* (9), he says that John wrote, 'asked by the bishops of Asia'. Almost the first account of the New Testament books is called the Muratorian Canon (*c.* A.D. 170). It says that John in his old age was asked to set down the story. They decided to fast and to pray to see what they should do. The divine revelation came that 'with all of them reviewing it, John should write all things in his own name'. The tradition always is that the Fourth Gospel was a community.

When the Fourth Gospel was written John must have been very old. He could not well have been less than ninety. Now when we turn to the Second and Third Letters of John we see that they were written by *the elder* (2 John 1; 3 John 1). There was a writer called Papias, who lived A.D. 60-130 approximately. He collected every possible bit of information about Jesus and the Gospels that he could—and he tells us that one of his sources was John the Elder.

So in Ephesus at the turn of the century there was John the Elder and John the Apostle; and the best explanation is that it was John the Elder who actually wrote the Fourth Gospel, in the sense that he was the penman, but that the material in it is the memory and the recollections of John the Apostle, who was the Beloved Disciple. It is John the Apostle, we believe, who is the source behind the Fourth Gospel, though the penman, as in the Second and Third Letters, was very probably John the Elder.

We must always remember that the Fourth Gospel was the last Gospel to be written; it was written about A.D. 100, and it was written in Ephesus. Out of this situation there come three things.

1. There had been time to remember—seventy years, and time to remember under the guidance of the Holy Spirit. Jesus had said to them that he had many things to say, which at the moment they could not bear, but which the Holy Spirit would bring them; he promised that the Holy Spirit would interpret in due time what he had said (John 16: 12, 15).

One feature of the Fourth Gospel is the long speeches. For instance John 6: 25-45 is Jesus speaking practically all the time. No one could expect a verbatim report after seventy years, in an age when people did not write things down as we do. We have already seen the tradition which said that John was to write, 'all of them reviewing it'. Beyond a doubt what happened was that John said: 'You remember how Jesus said?' and they said, 'Yes, and now we know what he meant.' And down went the saying by John and the interpretation by the Holy Spirit—exactly as Jesus had promised. The long speeches of Jesus in the Fourth Gospel are the work of the Holy Spirit thinking through the mind of John, after seventy years of remembering and of living with the risen Lord.

2. There had been time to think—seventy years of thinking. And the more they thought of Jesus the more wonderful he became. When Mark wrote about Jesus, he introduced Jesus full-grown, a man. When Matthew wrote about Jesus, he went back to Abraham (Matthew 1: 1). When Luke wrote about Jesus, he went back to Adam (Luke 3: 38). But when John wrote about Jesus, he went back to before time began (John 1: 1-3). The more they thought of Jesus, the more they saw him integrated into the purposes, the eternal purposes, of God.

But there is another thing in John. It has been pointed out that the Jew thinks in flash-points; modern man thinks in terms of dynamic process. For instance, the Jew sees creation happening in the flash-point of a week; modern man sees it as a divine, dynamic process still, after billions of years, going on.

John is by far the most modern of the New Testament writers. Take the idea of the Second Coming. Mostly the New Testament writers made it a flash-point somewhere in the future. John writes: 'If a man loves me, he will keep my word, and my Father will love him *and we will come to him and make our home with him*' (John 14: 23). For John there was at least a sense in which the Second Coming happened every time Jesus Christ comes in the Spirit into the heart of a man. Jesus comes again in his Spirit.

Take the case of judgment. Most people relegate judgment to a distant flash-point—but not John. 'Truly, truly, I say to you, he who hears my word and believes him who sent me, *has* eternal life; *he does not come into judgment, but has passed from death to life*' (John 5: 24). Judgment is a dynamic process going on every time a man is confronted with Jesus Christ.

3. Greatest of all, the Fourth Gospel meets the challenge to communicate the Gospel, seventy years on, in the Greek city of Ephesus. It was impossible to talk to the Greeks about a Son of David or a Messiah; these were Jewish ideas of which the Greek knew nothing. So the John of the Fourth Gospel was responsible for the greatest experiment in religious communication the world has ever seen. He presented Jesus as the *Logos*. Logos means both *word* and *reason* in Greek.

(a) In the creation story in Genesis 1 it is God's *word* which created. 'And God *said* . . .' Jesus is the Word, the re-creating Word come to men.

(b) A word is both the means of communication, and the expression of a thought. Jesus is the Word—God's means of communication to men—the very expression of God's thought.

(c) *Logos* for the Greek meant *reason*. The *Logos* was the mind of God interpenetrated through the universe, making sense of what could have been a chaos, and order out of disorder. 'All things,' said the Greeks, 'happen according to the *Logos*.' John said: 'Very well! The mind of God has come! The *Logos* has become flesh (John 1: 14). The mind of God has become a person.'

In one sentence, the supreme message of the Fourth Gospel is—If you want to see what God is like, look at Jesus. The Fourth Gospel is so modern that we have not caught up with it yet.

Questions for discussion

1. John used the ideas and conceptions of his own day to get the message of the Gospel across. Should we do the same today? If so, what ideas and conceptions could we use?

2. John was not in the least afraid to restate the Christian message in terms which would appeal to Ephesus in A.D. 100. Are we sometimes, or even often, too afraid to break away from language and from ideas which have ceased to mean anything to modern man?

3. John's Gospel was a community production. The Roman Catholic Church insists that the Bible cannot be studied or interpreted outside the tradition and the community of the Church. Would you agree that it is more profitable to study the Bible in fellowship with other Christians than alone? What steps are you taking to embark on such study in fellowship?

4. Now that you have studied the first three Gospels and the Fourth Gospel, wherein do you think that the Fourth differs from the other three? Which do you prefer: the Synoptic Gospels, or the Fourth Gospel?

Further reading
Commentaries by William Barclay (*Daily Study Bible*), R. V. G. Tasker (*Tyndale*), G. H. C. Macgregor (*Moffatt*), W. F. Howard (*Duckworth*), A. M. Hunter (*S.C.M.*).

5 · The message of the Church

The Acts of the Apostles

It would be possible to claim that Acts is the most important book in the New Testament, because without Acts we would know nothing whatever about the history of the first days of the Christian Church, except what we could deduce from the letters of Paul.

Without Acts the early history of the Church would be wrapped in darkness. If even two of the first three Gospels had been lost, in the one remaining Gospel we would still possess a real picture of Jesus; but if Acts had been lost the early history of the Church would have been a blank. And yet we have to look with some care at the title of this book. In both the Authorised Version and the Revised Standard Version it is titled *The Acts of the Apostles.* That is a title which promises far more than the book gives. From that title we would expect a comprehensive account of the careers of the twelve apostles.

In point of fact we have in Acts some account of the work of Peter; one brief sentence which tells of the death of James the brother of John (Acts 12: 2); some information about James the brother of Jesus who was not a member of the original twelve; a great deal about Paul, who also was not one of the original twelve; and John is mentioned, but he never utters one word. This is certainly not an account of the acts of the apostles.

The New English Bible removes the first *The*, and entitled the book *Acts of the Apostles*, which is better; but in the best

29

version of the title in Greek there are no articles at all. Both articles should be removed, and the title of the book ought to be simply *Acts of Apostolic Men*.

There are two ways to write history. An historian may attempt to give a day to day, week by week, month by month, year by year account of events. He may try for completeness, trying to write down in sequence everything that happened. Or, he may open a series of windows which look in on great significant moments.

It is the second way in which Luke works in Acts; he does not even try to give us a complete history of events. He sets before us a selection of significant events in the history of the Church. And in this selection three aims stand out.

1. There is a *political* aim. Luke wrote in the days when the threat of persecution hung over the Church, and his aim is to show not only that Christianity is politically innocent and morally blameless, but also that time and time again the Roman magistrates affirmed their belief that there was nothing in Christianity to condemn. In Corinth, Gallio declares that there is no wrong-doing or crime with which the Christians may be charged (Acts 18: 14). In Ephesus, the Recorder disperses the mob with the statement that the Christians are neither sacrilegious nor blasphemers (Acts 19: 37). The tribune Claudius Lysias writes to Felix that in his opinion Paul has done nothing to deserve imprisonment (Acts 23: 29). Festus tells Agrippa that, so far as he can see, Paul has done nothing to deserve death (Acts 25: 25). Agrippa and Festus and Berenice are agreed that, if Paul had not appealed to Caesar, he might well have gone free (Acts 26: 32).

More than once, in Philippi and in Jerusalem, Paul claims the rights of a Roman citizen (Acts 16: 35-40); 22: 25-29). And on the last journey to Rome the Roman centurion treats Paul with such courtesy and respect that, in the peril of the storm,

Paul becomes to all intents and purposes the leader of the party (Acts 27: 3-44).

It has even been suggested that Acts is the lawyer's brief for the defence of Paul in court. What is certainly true is that one of the main aims of Acts is to show that the Christians are morally and politically blameless.

2. There is an *historical* aim. The command of the Risen Christ is that the disciples are to be his witness in Jerusalem and in Judaea and in Samaria and to the ends of the earth (Acts 1: 8); and that is exactly the pattern which Acts follows. It shows Christianity going out in ever widening circles from Jerusalem to the ends of the earth.

3. There is a *theological* aim. It is clear in Acts that this expansion is no human achievement. One hundred and twenty ordinary men are told to go out and to convert the world (Acts 1: 15). Acts is the history of the power and energy of the Risen Christ in action. Luke's Gospel tells what Jesus Christ *began* to do; Acts 1: 1 tells of what he *continued* to do in his risen power. There is never a decision in Acts which is not taken under the guidance of the Spirit, and all the leaders of the Church are men of the Spirit.

The disciples are to wait in Jerusalem until the Spirit comes (Acts 1: 4, 5). The Spirit does come at Pentecost (Acts 2). The qualification of the office-bearers is that they are to be men of the Spirit (Acts 6: 3). It is the Spirit who tells Philip to make contact with the Ethiopian eunuch (Acts 8: 29). It is the Spirit who tells the Church at Antioch to send out Barnabas and Paul (Acts 13: 2). It is the Spirit who leads the Church to open its doors to the Gentiles (Acts 15: 28). It is the Spirit who guides the footsteps of Paul to Europe (Acts 16: 6, 7). Luke aims to show the Church as Spirit-guided and Spirit-powered.

Most important of all Acts shows us the kind of Gospel the early preachers preached. We must confine ourselves to Paul's three great missionary sermons at Antioch in Pisidia (Acts 13: 26-41); at Lystra (Acts 14: 15-17); at Athens (Acts 17: 22-31).

The first thing that strikes is how Paul suited his sermon to the audience. In the synagogue in Antioch he cites the Old Testament repeatedly, for they knew and loved the Old Testament there. In Lystra, in the backwoods, he cites no book at all; he begins from the wind and the rain and the growing things. In Athens, where no one knew anything about the Old Testament, he quotes their own poets to the Greeks.

Paul was a great preacher, because he began where his audience was, and with what they knew. He began with the here and now to get to the there and then. Let us look at the main lines of Paul's preaching.

1. To Paul everything that went before was a leading up to Jesus Christ. In history God was preparing for Christ (Acts 13: 16-26); in nature God was calling on men to remember himself (Acts 14: 15-17); even the inadequate religions of the heathen were preparations for the coming of Christ (Acts 17: 22-27). History, nature, the seeking mind of man find their climax in Christ.

2. With Jesus Christ the new age dawned, and all the prophecies of God came true. This is Peter's great conviction (Acts 2: 14-21). If we can even talk of such a thing as prophecy, then history is no knotless thread, no random succession of unrelated moments, history is the arena of the action of God.

3. When Jesus came they killed him; that too was foretold in prophecy (Acts 13: 29). The Cross is at one and the same time the greatest crime in history and part of the purpose of God (Acts 2: 23).

4. There is no sermon in Acts without triumph of the Resurrection. As has been well said, for them the Resurrection was the star in the firmament of the faith (Acts 13: 30-37; 17: 31). They did not preach on the Resurrection on Easter

Sunday only; they preached on it every Sunday in the year.

5. Through Jesus Christ there come the forgiveness of sins and the gift of the Spirit (Acts 13: 38, 39; 2: 38). This is to say, in the forgiveness the guilt and burden of the past are cancelled, and in the Spirit the demands of the future are met. In Jesus Christ there is a salvation from the past and a salvation for the future.

6. With the offer of forgiveness there went a threat to those who rejected it (Acts 13: 40, 41). The Saviour Christ is also Christ the Judge (Acts 17: 31). The early preaching had a threat in it. As Bunyan had it, a man can leave his sins and go to heaven, or keep his sins and go to hell.

7. Again and again in the early preaching there sounds the conviction that the hour has struck (Acts 13: 41; 14: 15-17; 17: 30). Maybe God before has held his hand; maybe men before could plead ignorance. But in Christ the hour has struck, God has acted, and, confronted with him, men must say 'yes' or 'no' to God.

Such was the preaching of the early Church, preaching in which the promise and the threat were strangely mingled, preaching in which men were confronted with the greatest offer in the world, and warned of the greatest danger in the world, preaching in which decision was demanded. If we would study the preaching and the history of the early Church, it is to Acts that we must go.

Questions for discussion

1. In Acts, Peter's sermons are in 1: 16-22; 2: 14-40; 3: 12-26; 4: 9-12; 10: 34-43; 11: 5-17. Paul's sermons are in 13: 16-41; 14: 15-17; 17: 22-31; 20: 18-35; 22: 1-21; 24: 10-21; 26: 2-23. Stephen's sermon is in Acts 7: 1-53. Read these sermons and discuss whether or not such preaching would be relevant and would get across today.

2. We saw that Paul varied his method to suit his audience, and that he always started where his listeners were. Where could preaching most effectively start today?

3. How effective is the argument from prophecy today? Is it effective at all? Note that Paul did not use it to any extent in Lystra or in Athens. Why?

4. Do you think that in modern preaching enough is made of (a) the guidance and power of the Holy Spirit, and (b) the demand for decision?

Further reading
Commentaries by William Barclay (*Daily Study Bible*), E. M. Blaiklock (*Tyndale*), R. R. Williams (*Torch*), R. B. Rackham (*Westminster*), F. F. Bruce (*Marshall, Morgan and Scott*), C. S. C. Williams (*A. and C. Black*).

6 · Faith alone

The Letter of Paul to the Romans

There will be none to dispute that the Letter to the Romans is Paul's greatest letter. Many great tributes have been paid to it. E. J. Goodspeed called it 'awe-inspiring'. Luther said of it, 'Romans contains in itself the plan of the whole scripture, and is a most complete epitome of the New Testament or Gospel.' Melanchthon, Luther's friend, called it 'a compendium of Christian doctrine'. To understand Romans is to go far towards understanding Paul.

When Paul wrote it, he was poised upon a great decision. One of Paul's dearest schemes was the collection for the church at Jerusalem from the younger churches (2 Corinthians 8 and 9). That collection had been made, and Paul was just about to leave for Jerusalem with it and with the delegates of the churches which had contributed to it (Acts 20: 4). But after the collection had been delivered, Paul had a plan. It was his purpose to visit Spain (Romans 15: 24-29).

Spain in the far west was a new territory for Paul, and, if he was to launch an invasion of Spain for Christ, he needed a base of operations, and the natural basis was Rome. Paul had always been haunted by Rome. When he set out on his last journey to Jerusalem, he says: 'After I have been there, I must see Rome also' (Acts 19: 21). When the clouds were gathering during the last days in Jerusalem, the Lord stood by him in the night, and said to him: 'Take courage, for as you have

35

testified about me at Jerusalem, so you must bear witness also at Rome' (Acts 23: 11). Paul was well aware that the journey to Rome was fraught with danger (Romans 15: 30-33). In point of fact, it ended in his arrest, and in the imprisonment from which he was never to be set free. He never reached Spain; he never paid that visit to Rome; it was as a prisoner under arrest that some time later he was to reach Rome.

But Paul, when he wrote the Letter to the Romans, had never been in Rome. He wanted Rome as a basis for his dreamed of expedition to Spain. And therefore he wrote to the Church at Rome a letter setting out his faith, so that they might see what kind of a man he was, and what kind of a faith he held, and so be ready to help and support him, when he set out for the far west.

In Romans, Paul concentrates on two closely related subjects—the relationship of man to God, and the relationship of man to man. In the Gentile world the relationship between God and man had broken down. The first chapter of Romans is a terrible indictment of the pagan world with its false wisdom, its idolatry, its homosexuality, and its immorality (Romans 1: 18-32). Nor was the Jewish world any better. The Jews have the law, and the law is holy, just and good, but they have it only to disobey it (Romans 2). All have sinned, and all fall short of the glory of God (Romans 3: 23). Sin's grip is on the world. And the trouble is that the law, which was designed to be a defence from sin, can be the very thing that kindles sin.

This is the subject of that piece of tortured biography in Romans 7. 'Apart from the law sin lies dead. . . . When the commandment came, sin revived and I died; the very commandment which promised life proved to be death to me' (Romans 7: 8-10). 'If it had not been for the law, I should not have known sin. I should not have known what it is to covet, if the law had not said, "You shall not covet"' (Romans 7: 7).

The trouble is that the law does two things. First, the law defines sin; it lays down what sin is. But second, no sooner is a thing forbidden than it is desired—this is the way of human nature—and therefore, by a tragic paradox, the law begets sin. Turn to the Gentile world, turn to the Jewish world, sin is in control.

But the matter is worse than that. It is in Romans that we meet the doctrine of original sin. Original sin does not mean the tendency to sin; it does not mean an inherited predisposition to sin; it means quite and totally literally that in Adam all sinned—you and I sinned. This is the ancient conception of solidarity. We are individualists; but in the ancient world the individual hardly existed. A man thought of himself, not as an individual, but as a member of a family, a clan, a nation. When Achan sinned, they killed him and his sons and his daughters and his animals and killed them all (Joshua 7). So the doctrine of the original sin holds that because of this solidarity all men literally sinned in Adam.

The basis of the doctrine is in Romans 5: 12-14. It can be outlined in a series of steps.

1. The cause of death is sin.

2. Adam disobeyed a positive command of God, the command not to eat of the forbidden tree.

3. Therefore Adam died.

4. Where there is no law to break there can be no sin.

5. Between Adam and Moses the law did not yet exist, because God had not yet given the law.

6. Although there was no law to break between Adam and Moses men continued to die.

7. Why? Because all men had literally sinned in Adam, and therefore all had to die.

What is to happen? Man, Jew and Gentile, is helpless. So God in Jesus Christ steps in. If there can be solidarity with

Adam, there can be solidarity with Jesus Christ. If man is identified with the sin of Adam, he can be identified with the obedience of Jesus Christ. The terrible process begun in Adam can be reversed in Christ (Romans 5: 15-21).

How can this be? By faith. And what is faith? Faith is doing what Abraham did—it is taking God at his word (Romans 4: 16-25), accepting God's commands, believing in God's promises, certain that God means, and can do, what he says? And faith is far older than circumcision and the law, for Abraham was right with God before ever he was circumcised and centuries before the law was given to Moses. So God comes to each man, and says in Jesus Christ: 'Take me at my word.'

What happens when we take God at his word? When that happens we are *justified*. It is clear that Paul is using the word *justify* in a special sense. He talks of God as the one who justifies the ungodly (Romans 4: 5). If in modern language I justify myself or some one else, I produce reasons to prove that I or the other person was right to act as I or he did. Now God is not going to produce reasons to prove that the sinner is right to be a sinner.

What then does *justify* mean? In Greek the verb to *justify* is *dikaioun*. Greek verbs which end in -*oun* do not mean to make a person something; they mean to treat, reckon or account someone as something. So when it is said that God justifies the sinner it means that *God treats the sinner as if he had been a good man*. It means that though we are hell-deserving sinners God still loves us; it means that not even our sin can separate us from God. It means, in a word, that the relationship between us and God is the relationship between father and son in Jesus' parable of the Prodigal Son.

To be justified by faith is to take God at his word that for the sake of Jesus Christ he will treat me as a beloved son, sinner though I am, if I come to him (Romans 3 and 4). This is what we mean by the *grace* of God. And now there is another problem which Paul deals with in Romans 6. 'Are we to continue in sin that grace may abound?' (Romans 6: 1). Someone comes to Paul and says: 'You say that God's grace is the greatest thing in the world?' 'Yes'. 'You say that God's grace can forgive any sin?' 'Yes.'

Then comes the answer: 'If that is so, let's go on sinning, for the more we sin, the more chances we give this wonderful grace to operate. Sin is a good thing for sin produces grace.' Paul's answer is that to speak like that is to show that we do not know what Christianity is all about. For Paul, baptism was adult baptism and baptism was instructed baptism and baptism was, if possible, baptism by immersion.

In baptism (Romans 6: 3-11) we, as it were, die with Christ, when we plunge below the water, and rise with him, when we rise from the water; and thus we leave the old life behind, and set out on a life that is new. To put it much more simply, how can wo go on sinning, when we look at the cross, and say: 'God loved me like that?'

Romans chapters 9 to 11 deal with another of the great problems, the problem of why the Jews rejected the Messiah when he came and the problem of their ultimate fate. In chapter 9 Paul begins with the grim statement that the Jews rejected the Messiah, because God willed it and arranged it so; but that is not the end of the story. For he goes on to show that the plan of God is that in the end the Gentiles should bring in the Jews, and that in the end of the day all would be saved. 'God has consigned all men to disobedience that he may have mercy on all' (Romans 11: 32). Temporary rejection was designed to end in universal salvation.

In chapters 12 to 15 Paul turns to the ethical duty of the Christian, and shows men their duty to each other, their duty to the state, and their duty to the weaker brother. The soaring theology of the first eleven chapters is in Paul's invariable way brought to the service of everyday work and life and living.

So in this greatest of letters Paul lays down the way to a right relationship with God and a right relationship with each other.

Questions for discussion

1. Can a modern man really accept the doctrine of original sin in the form in which Paul presents it? What is the essential truth which that doctrine really stands for?

2. In Romans 9 Paul uses the analogy of the potter (Romans 9: 19-23). He takes it from Jeremiah 18: 1-6. Is this really a satisfactory analogy? Can we think of God making and breaking men as a potter makes and breaks the vessels made of clay? Can we believe that God will ever treat men as *things* to be made and broken as he wishes? Does this agree with the idea of God as father?

3. What do we mean by faith? How much of faith consists in believing that certain things are true (accepting a creed), and how much of faith consists in believing in a person (believing that what Jesus says and claims is true)? How much of faith is intellectual, and how much of faith is encounter with, and committal to, a person?

4. Read Romans 12, 13, 14, 15 and work out what a Christian's duty is (a) to the community; (b) to the state; (c) to the weaker brother; (d) to the person who holds different opinions from his.

Further reading

Commentaries by William Barclay (*Daily Study Bible*), F. F. Bruce (*Tyndale*), C. H. Dodd (*Moffatt*), C. K. Barrett (*A. and C. Black*), K. E. Kirk (*Clarendon*).

7 · The pastor and his problems

The First Letter of Paul to the Corinthians

It has been said that the First Letter to the Corinthians takes the roof off the early Church and enables us to see what was going on inside. No letter shows us so much of the problems of the pastor. There are so many problems and answers that in this study we can do no more than state each one and its solution in a sentence or two.

Corinth was a city of 200,000 citizens and 500,000 slaves. It was one of the greatest commercial cities of the ancient world. Greece is almost cut in two by the Corinthian and the Saronic Gulfs. Between them they leave an isthmus of no more than five miles wide and on that isthmus Corinth stands. Corinth was quite literally the bridge of Greece, and through it every single item of Greek north-to-south trade had to pass. Further, the extreme tip of southern Greece, Cape Malea, was a dangerous place, as dangerous as Cape Horn. 'Let him who sails round Malea forget his home and make his will,' the Greeks said.

So what happened was that the east-to-west traffic of the Mediterranean sailed up one of the gulfs. If the ship was small enough, it was put on rollers and hauled over to the other side; if the ship was too large for that, the cargo was unloaded and carried across to a ship on the other side. Thus a very large proportion of the east-to-west trade of the Mediterranean passed through Corinth. Corinth was the Piccadilly Circus of the traffic of the Mediterranean. Corinth was 'wealthy Corinth'.

But Corinth was also one of the worst cities in the ancient world. Above it on the Acrocorinthus stood the Temple of Aphrodite, which had more than a thousand priestesses, who were sacred prostitutes. To have intercourse with one of these girls was an act of worship. So they came down to the city at evening and plied their trade, until it was a proverb, 'Not every man can afford a journey to Corinth.' A 'Corinthian maid' was a Greek synonym for a prostitute. The Greek verb *korinthiazesthai* means to pander or to play the harlot. The word *Corinthian* came into English to describe the Regency bucks and debauches. Aelian tells us that in stage plays a Corinthian was never brought on to the stage any other way than drunk.

Such was Corinth. 'The Church of God which is at Corinth'—a huge and happy paradox, Bengel called that phrase—the family of God among the godless.

In 6: 9-11 Paul makes a list of sinners and then triumphantly ends 'and such were some of you'. In Corinth Christianity worked, for in Corinth Christianity made bad men good. Paul received his information about what was going on in Corinth from three sources. He was in Ephesus when he wrote. He got it from Chloe's people (1: 11). He got it from a letter the Corinthians had written him (7: 1). He got it from Stephanas, Fortunatus and Achaicus, who had come to visit him (16: 17). No fewer than eleven different problems had arisen.

1. *The problems of the partisan spirit* (1: 10, 11; 3: 3-15). Some claimed Apollos as their leader, some Peter, some Paul. Apollos was an Alexandrian intellectual (Acts 18: 24), and no doubt those who claimed him were the Corinthian intellectuals. There is a tradition that Peter had visited Corinth. Perhaps those who claimed him traced their conversion to him, and were the equivalent of old-fashioned evangelicals. Those who

claimed Paul no doubt stood for Christian freedom and liberty to do as they liked. Very likely what Paul is saying in 1: 12 is: 'You say you belong to Paul or to Apollos or to Cephas—*I belong to Christ*.' The Church is not the Church of any man; it is the Church of Christ.

2. *The problems of intellectual pride* (1: 17, 20-25; 2: 1-5, 10-16; 3: 18-23). In Corinth Paul had been determined to know only Jesus Christ and Jesus Christ on his Cross (2: 2). It is not without significance that Paul came straight from Athens to Corinth. In Athens, Paul had made his one 'philosophic' speech—and it had been a failure (Acts 17: 22-34). In Corinth, Paul was more concerned with God's revelation in Jesus Christ than with man's intellect and what it could do. True, the revelation would have to be thought out; but first it had to be accepted.

3. *The problem of immorality* (ch. 5). A man was cohabiting with his stepmother, and the congregation had done nothing about it. It has been said that chastity was the one completely new virtue Christianity brought into the world. The Corinthian Christians were like an island of morality in a sea of paganism. They were only one remove from their old life, and infection and contamination were desperately easy. Paul pleads for Christian discipline. He is clear that out in the world the Christian cannot separate himself from the immoral man, or he could not enter the world at all. But inside the Church the standards must be observed.

4. *The problem of legal disputes* (6: 1-8). For Greeks going to law with each other was one of life's commonest recreations; they were the most litigious people the world has ever seen. Paul demands that they live at peace and that, if differences do arise, they should be settled within the fellowship of the Church. Whatever may be true of modern life, for Paul it was true that the Christian does not engage in personal law-suits.

5. *There was the problem of antinomianism* (6: 9-20). In Greece there was a point of view that matter is essentially evil and that only spirit is good. If that be so, the body is essentially evil. 'The body,' said Plato, 'is the prison-house of the soul.' 'I am a poor soul,' said Epictetus, 'shackled to a corpse.' Seneca spoke of 'the detestable habitation of the body.' So, it was argued, if the body is bad, do what you like with it. You can't make it worse than it is. Sate it, glut it; it makes no difference. Paul's answer is that man is not body *or* soul; he is body *and* soul; and both have been redeemed by Jesus Christ and both belong to God, and both can be inhabited by the Spirit. A clean soul in a clean body, for both belong to Christ.

6. So far Paul has been answering the information brought by Chloe's people. Now he proceeds to answer the Corinthians' letter to him. *There are the problems of marriage and of sexual relations* (ch. 7). There is no doubt that, if Paul had edited his own letters, he would have severely edited this chapter. In it he teaches that marriage is no more than a second best, only to be entered into if a man has not the continence to remain pure, and that sexual relations are something that life would be better without. But this is so because at this time Paul's one conviction is that 'the time is very short' (7: 29). He was expecting the Second Coming at any moment, and he wanted absolute concentration on Jesus Christ (7: 32-35). He came to see that the human situation was much more permanent than he had thought, and his last word on marriage is in Ephesians 5: 21-33, where the relationship between husband and wife is likened to the relationship between Christ and the Church.

7. *The problem of meat offered to idols* (chs. 8-10). The problem was this. Usually only a token part of a victim was burned on the altar. A portion of it went to the worshipper and a portion went to the priest. With his portion the worshipper

often gave a party, and very often the party was in the temple of the heathen god. Part of the priests' share—they got more than they could eat—ended in the shops. The trouble was that, if a person was going to refuse to eat meat offered to idols, he would go far to cutting himself off completely from social fellowship.

Paul has more than one thing to say. The hands that touched the body of Christ in the sacrament cannot touch meat offered to an idol. A man may have so strong a faith that he just does not think it matters, but the weaker brother has a tender conscience, and for the sake of the weak the strong must yield, and out of this apparently recondite argument there comes the great principle: 'If food is a cause of my brother's falling, I will never eat meat, lest I cause my brother to fall' (8: 13). Never was Christian responsibility better stated.

8. *The problem of women in the Church* (11: 1-16; 14: 34-36). The problem is whether women are to be veiled or not. The background of this is very simple. In the ancient world, if a woman was veiled, no one would speak to her or molest her. If she went without a veil, she was declaring herself a loose woman, and any man felt free to accost her. Further, the respectable Greek wife and her mother lived a completely secluded life; she did not even eat with the family if strange men were present. As for Jewish law, under it a woman was a thing and had no rights at all, not even the right to be educated. When we read passages like this, we must remember that it is to Christianity that women owe their emancipation, and all that happened in Corinth was that women in the early Church, or at least some of them, wanted to go too far too fast. They were demanding a liberty which *at that moment*—not now—would have got the Church a bad name.

9. *There was the problem of the Lord's Supper* (11: 17-34). At that time the Lord's Supper was in part a common meal called

the Love Feast. It ought to have been a real act of fellowship. Instead of that the rich gorged and the poor starved and fellowship was killed (11: 18-22). Their fault was that they ate and drank *without discerning the body* (11: 29). *Note* that the phrase 'not discerning the *Lord's* body' is not in the RSV—and the RSV is correct—it is simply *not discerning the body;* and it means that, if we sit at the Lord's Table forgetting that we are one body in Christ, at variance with our fellow-men, we have no right to be there.

10. *The problem of spiritual gifts* (chs. 12-14). The Church, says Paul, is like a body. No two parts are the same, but no part is greater than any other part, and the Church is only healthy when each part does its duty. Then the Church becomes the body of Christ, the instrument and agent through which Jesus Christ can work. Chapter 14 is important. It describes the Church's worship. Prophesying here means proclaiming the word of God, and Paul is much in favour of it because it edifies the congregation, because they can understand. The gift of tongues is not the gift of speaking foreign languages, but the pouring out of a flood of unintelligible sounds in no known tongue in an ecstasy. Paul does not deny this gift, but he sets little store by it, because it is unintelligible (although it can be interpreted) and no man can be edified by what he cannot understand. The whole direction of these chapters is that the really important things are not the recondite and spectacular things, but the ordinary work of every day.

11. *The problem of the resurrection of the body* (ch. 15). It is not the immortality of the soul that is in question—the Greek believed in that—it is the resurrection of the body. It is put in this way because Greek has no word for *personality*. What Paul is pleading is that man is saved both body and soul, and that after death you will still be you and I will still be I. The individual will remain. The resurrection body will be no more

like this body than the golden waving corn is like the shrivelled seed from which it came or the daffodil like the bulb (15: 35-50). We would be better to say: 'I believe in the survival of personality', and to leave the matter of in what body to the wisdom of God.

Such then in brief summary were the problems of the pastor in Corinth, and they are full of guidance for the problems of today.

Questions for discussion

1. 'Preaching is truth through personality.' How can we recognise this fact and make use of it, and at the same time keep the personality of the preacher from obtruding too much?

2. Are there some people temperamentally able to accept things, while others feel that they must understand as well as accept? How can we combine simplicity of belief with depth of thought? Do you think that temperament enters into this question?

3. What are your views about Church discipline? Should there be discipline? Who should exercise it? What form should it take?

4. Paul says that he will eat no meat if the eating of meat causes his brother to fall. What habits can we demand for ourselves which might be harmful to others? Are there any pleasures which a full sense of Christian responsibility might make it necessary to give up?

5. Read 1 Corinthians 14. In view of this chapter do you think that speaking with tongues is really something on which the Church should lay stress?

6. The Stoics believed that when a man died his soul was absorbed in the being of God. What difference is there between a belief like that and the Christian belief about the life to come?

Further reading
Commentaries by William Barclay (*Daily Study Bible*), C. K. Barrett (*A. and C. Black*), F. F. Bruce (*New Century Bible*), J. Héring, J. Moffatt (*Moffatt*), L. Morris (*Tyndale*), W. G. H. Simon (*Torch*).

8 · Strife and reconciliation

The Second Letter of Paul to the Corinthians

The Second Letter to the Corinthians is not nearly so connected a whole as the First Letter is, and there are reasons for that. Paul's letters were not edited and collected until about thirty years after his death. It slowly dawned on the Church, especially after the publication of Acts, what a spiritual giant Paul had been. So, bit by bit, his letters were collected and published. But thirty years is a long time, and sometimes the letters had been lost and sometimes they had been damaged and mutilated. Something like this happened to Paul's correspondence with the Church at Corinth. We certainly do not possess the whole of it, and what we have of it is very probably in the wrong order.

1. There quite certainly was a letter which precedes any of the letters which we now have. In 1 Corinthians 5: 9 Paul writes: 'I wrote to you in my letter not to associate with immoral men.' He does not mean out in the world, because, if in the day's work we had to associate only with good men, we would have to stay out of the world altogether. He means within the Church. This letter was written before 1 Corinthians. Is it altogether lost? There is just a chance that a bit of it is embedded in 2 Corinthians 6: 14 to 7: 1. In the RSV and in the NEB that passage is printed as a separate block of material with a space before it and a space after it, making it stand alone. It begins (RSV): 'Do not be mismated with unbelievers', and goes on to warn the Christian to avoid the company of

immoral men—which is exactly what the first letter was about. Further, if you take out 2 Corinthians 6: 14 to 7: 1 and read straight on from 6: 13 to 7: 2 you get excellent sense. It may well be that 2 Corinthians 6: 14 to 7: 1 is a page of the letter which is referred to in 1 Corinthians 5: 9, a page which got misplaced when the letters were collected.

2. Next there comes 1 Corinthians, which we have already studied, and which deals with the news brought by Chloe's people (1 Corinthians 1: 11) in chapters 1-6; and then with answers to a letter which the Corinthians had written to Paul in chapters 7-16.

3. 1 Corinthians was sent off with Timothy. 'I am sending to you Timothy,' Paul writes, 'my beloved and faithful child in the Lord, to remind you of my ways in Christ (1 Corinthians 4: 17). 'When Timothy comes, see that you put him at ease among you. . . . Speed him on his way in peace, that he may return to me' (1 Corinthians 16: 10). So 1 Corinthians is written and despatched with Timothy.

4. From the point of view of mending the situation this letter was a complete failure. And so Paul paid a flying visit to Corinth. There is no actual record of that visit, but it must have been paid. In 2 Corinthians 12: 14 Paul writes: 'For the *third* time I am ready to come to you.' The only visit recorded is the long stay in Acts 18: 1-18, but if a third visit was contemplated there must have been a second. In 2 Corinthians 13: 1, 2 Paul writes: 'This is the third time I am coming to you.' He says that on his second visit he warned them that if they did not mend their ways he would not spare them. It was clearly a painful visit.

5. Again, this visit did nothing to help, and so Paul wrote a very stern and severe letter. 'I wrote to you,' he says, 'out of much affliction and anguish of heart and with many tears' (2 Corinthians 2: 4). 'Even if I made you sorry with my letter

I do not regret it (though I did regret it), for I see that that letter grieved you, though only for a while. As it is, I rejoice, not because you were grieved, but because you were grieved into repenting' (2 Corinthians 7: 8, 9).

Have we got this sad, stern, severe letter? If you read straight through 2 Corinthians, you are aware of an extraordinary break at chapter 10. Up to the end of chapter 9 all is at peace, and then chapter 10 begins the most heart-broken heart's cry Paul ever wrote, in which it is made quite clear that Paul and his apostleship are under bitter attack. It is highly probable that 2 Corinthians 10-13 is the broken-hearted letter that Paul was compelled to write after the bitter visit.

6. This letter was sent off with Titus. Paul was so eager for an answer that he could not wait, and went to Troas to meet Titus. Titus had not arrived, so Paul pressed on to Macedonia to meet him (2 Corinthians 2: 13).

There in Macedonia he met him and learned that all was well (2 Corinthians 7: 5-13). And it was then that he wrote 2 Corinthians 1-9, which is the letter of reconciliation, when the breach was mended, and Paul and his people were one again.

So then, if we want to read the continued story of Corinth in the right order—and, when we do, it becomes even more gripping—we must follow this scheme.

1. The previous Letter in 2 Corinthians 6: 14 to 7: 1.

2. 1 Corinthians which is despatched by Timothy, and which fails to improve matters.

3. The sorrowful visit.

4. The severe letter which is in 2 Corinthians 10-13.

5. That letter was despatched by Titus, whom Paul met in Macedonia. There he learned that all was well, and thereupon wrote the letter of reconciliation which is in 2 Corinthians 1-9.

That is the real scenario of the Corinthian correspondence.

We wish to select only one thing out of the varied material in

2 Corinthians; and we select it because it was dear to Paul's heart, and because it has much relevance for the Church today. One of the very first things that Paul promised to do, when he became an accepted missionary of the Christian Church, was to remember the poor (Galatians 2: 10). That memory took one particular direction. One of Paul's dearest undertakings was to organise a collection from the younger Churches for the poor of the Church in Jerusalem. We find repeated references to this collection.

In 1 Corinthians 16: 1-4 he urges the Corinthians to give regularly and generously to the collection, so that it will be on time for delivery. In Romans 15: 26-28 he tells the Roman Church that he hopes to come to visit it on his way to Spain, but that he must first take the collection to Jerusalem. We read in Acts 24: 17 how Paul told Felix that the object of the journey to Jerusalem which led to his arrest was to bring alms and offerings to his own people. But it is in chapters 8 and 9 of 2 Corinthians that we learn most about this collection.

It had begun in the Churches of Macedonia, who out of their own poverty had given generously, and Paul appeals to the Corinthians to do the same. If they give, they but follow the example of their Lord, who for their sakes laid aside the riches of his glory and became poor (2 Corinthians 8: 1-15). Then Paul outlines the steps he has taken to demonstrate that the collection has been efficiently taken and honestly handled (2 Corinthians 8: 16-24). He wants them to have the collection made up to time, so that there will be no last minute rush, and so that the thing will clearly be seen as a gift and not as something unwillingly extracted (2 Corinthians 9: 1-5).

From the various references to the collection we can compile a set of principles for Christian liberality.

1. For a Christian to give is nothing less than an obligation (Romans 15: 27; Galatians 2: 10).

2. Even if the gift be handed to some official of the Church, it is nonetheless given to God (2 Corinthians 8: 5).

3. The pattern and example of giving is Jesus himself, who, though he was rich, for our sakes became poor (2 Corinthians 8: 9).

4. In such giving two things happen. (a) Love is turned into action and stops being mere words (2 Corinthians 8: 8). (b) The unity of the Church is demonstrated (2 Corinthians 8: 10-15), a unity in which it is impossible for some to have too much, while others have too little.

5. Certain laws of liberality emerge. Giving should be *regular* (1 Corinthians 16: 1, 2). Better a little regularly than a frantic search when the total sum becomes due.

6. It should be *proportionate* to a man's resources (1 Corinthians 16: 1, 2). A man is not asked to beggar himself; he is asked out of his surplus to help the man who has nothing at all (2 Corinthians 8: 12-15). There is no credit in leaving oneself destitute, and there should be no pleasure in leaving oneself in luxury.

7. It should be *willing* and joyous. It must not be given as an extortion. God loves a cheerful giver (2 Corinthians 9: 6-11). It must be universal and not left to the few.

8. Any gift to the poor is in fact a thanksgiving to God (2 Corinthians 9: 12). No man can show his gratitude to God better than by helping his fellowman.

9. The sight of such generosity and such a sense of responsibility for others is a powerful commendation of Christianity and brings glory to God (2 Corinthians 9: 13-15).

10. It is not without significance that Paul makes the most careful arrangements for the administration of the fund (2 Corinthians 8: 16-24). There must be no room for any suggestion of dishonesty.

11. It is again to be noted that arrangements are made to

have the gift personally delivered (2 Corinthians 8: 22-24). Even in those days a bank draft could have been sent, but, if it is possible, the giving must be person to person.

So then Paul has much to teach us about the duty and the method of Christian liberality.

Questions for discussion

1. It has been said: 'A Church is not a business, but there is no reason why it should not be run in a businesslike way.' Do you agree with this? Is this part of what Paul meant when he said: 'We intend that no one should blame us about this liberal gift which we are administering, for we aim at what is honourable, not only in the Lord's sight but also in the sight of men'? (2 Corinthians 8: 20, 21).

2. What do you think that giving in proportion to one's possessions should be? What kind of proportion would be right?

3. Are we ever guilty of having too much while others have too little? If so, what can we do about it?

4. What do you think of what is called 'indiscriminate charity'? Do you think that our giving should always be through official channels? Is there a place for personal giving?

Further reading
Commentaries by William Barclay (*Daily Study Bible*), R. V. G. Tasker (*Tyndale*), R. H. Strachan (*Moffatt*), F. F. Bruce (*New Century Bible*).

9 · Christian freedom

The Letter of Paul to the Galatians

Sir William Ramsay called the Letter to the Galatians 'the most remarkable letter that was ever written', and he was right because it was the Letter to the Galatians which begat the Reformation. It was the letter wherein Luther found faith for himself, and a new faith for the world. Luther said of this letter: 'The Epistle to the Galatians is my Epistle; I have betrothed myself to it; it is my wife.' 'This Epistle,' said Godet, 'marks an epoch in the history of man; it is the ever precious document of his spiritual emancipation.'

But not only have what we might call the public consequences of this letter been unique; it has also been unique as medicine for the sick soul. John Bunyan said of Luther's commentary on Galatians: 'God, in whose hand are all our days and ways, did cast into my hand one day a book of Martin Luther. It was his *Comment on the Galatians*. It was so old that it was ready to fall piece from piece, if I did but turn it over. . . . This, methinks, I must let fall before all men—I do prefer this book of Martin Luther upon the Galatians (excepting the Holy Bible) before all books that ever I have seen as most fit for a wounded conscience.' The book that is the charter of Christian freedom, the book that provided the dynamic of the Reformation, the book that has always brought health and comfort to the sick soul—this indeed is one of the supreme books of the world.

There has always been a doubt as to the people to whom

Galatians was written. The problem is that the word Galatians was used in two senses in New Testament times. Four hundred years before Jesus came there was one of the great migrations of history. The Galli came pouring over the northern mountain barriers into Europe. They were also called the Celts; their descendants and their language to this day survive in those who speak Gaelic, Erse, Welsh, Cornish and Breton.

They were a wild and terrifying people. In Asia Minor by 230 B.C. they had been confined to a strip of country in the north-east called Galatia, the kingdom of the Galli, whose three principal cities were Pessinus, Tavium and Ancyra. In 189 B.C. the Romans made them a protectorate, still under their own kings, but answerable to Rome. In 29 B.C. on the death of King Amyntas the final step was taken. They were completely incorporated into the Roman Empire, and Rome at the same time took the opportunity to make a reorganisation in which a new province was formed, consisting of the old kingdom of Galatia, of Lycaonia, Isauria, South-east Phrygia, parts of Pisidia, Pontus and Paphlagonia. And to the new province the name Galatia was given. So the name stood both for the ancient kingdom and for the new province.

There is no record of Paul ever having been in the ancient kingdom area, in Tavium, Pessinus and Ancyra. If he ever was, the only possible references are in Acts 16: 6-8 and 18: 23. On the other hand, we have a vivid story of what happened in Antioch in Pisidia, in Lystra, Derbe and Iconium, and they were all in the Roman province. It is much more likely that the name Galatia means the Roman province rather than the ancient kingdom, and that the background to the letter is to be found in the story of Acts 13 and 14.

One thing we do know. When Paul came to Galatia, he was a sick man. He was suffering from what in his second letter to the Corinthians he called the thorn in his flesh (2 Corinthians 12:

7). The word Paul uses for thorn is *skolops*, which means a stake rather than thorn. The pain of his trouble was not like a pinprick but like a stake turning and twisting in his body. What that thorn in the flesh was Paul in his reticence never told us, and there have been many speculations. It has been suggested that it was the constant opposition which he encountered. Many Roman Catholic commentators think that the thorn was sexual desire, which, they say, Paul never mastered. Some people think that Paul was an epileptic.

When he tells of his arrival in Galatia as a sick man (Galatians 4: 12-15), he says that in spite of his illness they did not scorn or *despise* him. The word he uses for *to despise* means literally *to spit at;* and in the ancient world it was the custom to spit when you saw an epileptic, in order to ward off the evil demon in him. The earliest suggestion, made away back in the fifth century, was that Paul suffered from eye trouble; and indeed he says that the Galatians were so grateful to him that they would have plucked out their eyes and given them to him, if it had been possible (Galatians 4: 15). He says, 'see with what large letters I am writing to you with my own hand' (Galatians 6: 11), which could be a reference to the large sprawling writing of a half-blind man.

Another very early suggestion was that Paul suffered from prostrating headaches, which might well go with the eye-trouble. The likeliest suggestion is that Paul suffered from chronic malaria which brings with it a headache which has been said to be like a red hot bar or a dentist's drill boring through the forehead. We do well to remember that Paul made his journeyings in pain—and talks very little about it, so little that we can only guess what the trouble was.

In the letter to the Galatians Paul was under attack. Gloel said of it: 'It is not a sermon, it is not a treatise; it is a sword-cut, delivered in the hour of extreme peril by a combatant assailed by dangerous foes.' W. M. Macgregor used to liken Galatians to 'a sword flashing in a great swordsman's hand'.

1. First of all, Paul's apostleship was under attack. In this matter Paul was vulnerable. He had not been one of the original Twelve. He had not been a witness of the resurrection in the first forty days after Jesus rose from the dead. In one sense he was no more than a renegade from Judaism (Galatians 1: 13), and above all there had been a time when he was a notorious persecutor of the Church (1: 13, 23). So Paul begins with a resounding hammer blow. He is an apostle, not from men, nor through man, but through Jesus Christ and God the Father (Galatians 1: 1), and that apostleship had been accepted as genuine by the great leaders of the Church (Galatians 2: 8-10). As an apostle, so he claimed, he was divinely appointed and humanly approved.

2. His gospel was under attack. Paul lays it down that the gospel he preached was not man's gospel (Galatians 1: 11).He owed it to no man's instruction (Galatians 1: 15-17) and, when the day did come, when he submitted that gospel of his to the church leaders, they were compelled to admit that they had nothing to add to what he already possessed (Galatians 2: 1-10). Like his apostleship, his gospel was divinely given and humanly approved.

3. But who was it who was attacking him? When we read the story in Acts, we see that his attackers were the Jews, in Antioch (Acts 13: 50, 51); in Iconium (Acts 14: 2); and in Lystra (Acts 14: 19). And the trouble was that they were Christian Jews. There were Jews who were completely hostile to Christianity, and there were Jews who completely accepted Christianity. But there were Jews in a middle position. They clung to the conviction that the Jews were the chosen people; they regarded Jesus as the Jewish Messiah, and, if he was the Messiah, he was the possession of the Jewish race; and therefore

they held that, before a man could enjoy the blessings of Christianity, he must become a Jew; that is to say, he must be circumcised and accept the Jewish ceremonial law about food and drink and all the rest of it. And when they found Paul opening the door to all and sundry on faith alone, they were infuriated.

4. What then was Paul's answer? First, he argued from experience. It was in fact by hearing with faith, not by works of the law, that they had received the Spirit (Galatians 3: 1-5). Second, he argued from prophecy. Had not the prophet said: 'He who through faith is righteous shall live. The just shall live by faith' (Habakkuk 2: 4; Galatians 3: 11)? He argued from history. When Abraham was accepted by God, he was not circumcised, and in point of fact it was not until four hundred and thirty years later that the Law was given (Galatians 3: 10-18). Experience, prophecy, history—all prove that the way to right relationships with God is faith.

5. What then is the use of the law? The law defines sin, and by defining sin, drives a man to despair. The law, he says, is what the AV calls our schoolmaster, and the RSV our custodian, to bring us to Christ (Galatians 3: 19-29). The word is *paidagogos*. The *paidagogos* had nothing to do with the actual education of the child. His duty was to see the child safely through the streets, to bring him to the door of the school, to hand him over to the master, and then to withdraw. The law with its demands could drive a man to despair and so drive him to Christ—but that was all it could do.

6. And lastly, what was basically wrong with this Jewish attack?

(a) It was asking the Christian to give up a religion of freedom to return to a religion of law (Galatians 5: 1). The Christian is not the slave of the law: he is the free man of the Spirit. Nor is his freedom licence, for Christian freedom is guided by the Spirit, controlled by love, and bounded by responsibility (Galatians 5: 13-26).

(b) And there was something worse. If a man believed he had to get himself circumcised, and if he believed that he must accept the law, then by these very actions he was saying that what Christ had done for him was not enough, that to the work of Christ there must be added some works that he must offer (Galatians 5: 2-11; 6: 11-16).

What Paul is proclaiming is the total adequacy of what Jesus had done on the Cross. It is folly for a man to try to save himself, or to try to add to what Jesus Christ has done. If a man has faith, if he commits himself totally to the mercy of God in utter trust in what Jesus has done for him—that is enough. No man can achieve merit; he can only accept mercy. And, if he accepts mercy, he will know that freedom which moves in the realm of the Spirit, and which is beyond the legalism of law.

Questions for discussion

1. Are there still signs of legalism in the religion which some people practise today?

2. Discuss how Christian love and Christian responsibility control Christian freedom. What kind of things would they prevent us from doing?

3. Discuss Luther's saying that the Christian is at one and the same time the freest of all men and the servant of all men.

4. Do we ever think in terms of earning salvation? Think out the difference between good works which are done to earn merit and good works which are done to show gratitude.

Further reading
Commentaries by William Barclay (*Daily Study Bible*), R. A. Cole (*Tyndale*), G. S. Duncan (*Moffatt*), Donald Guthrie (*New Century Bible*).

10 · The function of the Church

The Letter of Paul to the Ephesians

Of the greatness of the Letter to the Ephesians there has never been any doubt. It has been called, and rightly, 'The Queen of the Epistles'.

When John Knox was dying, the book that was most often read to him was John Calvin's *Sermons on the Letter to the Ephesians*. Coleridge said of the Letter to the Ephesians that it is 'the divinest composition of man'. He went on to give his reasons for this high verdict: 'It embraces, first, those doctrines peculiar to Christianity and, then, those precepts common with it in natural religion.'

God revealed in Christ and God revealed in his world both have their place in the message of Ephesians. But, especially in the RSV, Ephesians begins by presenting us with a problem. The RSV (Ephesians 1: 2) omits the word Ephesus altogether, and addresses the letter to: 'The saints who are also faithful in Christ Jesus'. According to the RSV this letter is not really the Letter to the Ephesians at all. What causes this doubt? There are three main reasons.

1. Ephesians is the most impersonal letter Paul ever wrote. There is no mention of any particular local situation. No one is named in it except Tychicus the bearer of it (6: 21). All that Paul can say is that he has *heard* of their faith and love (1: 15). He feels that he can assume that they have *heard* of the stewardship of God's grace for the Gentiles which was given

to him (3: 2). There is a kind of remoteness about this. He has *heard* of them and they have *heard* of him; the very way of speaking seems to imply that there was no personal contact.

And yet the fact is that Paul spent the better part of three years in Ephesus (Acts 19: 9, 10), and on his last meeting with the elders of the Ephesian congregation he made one of the most intimately emotional farewell speeches any man could ever make (Acts 20: 17-35). It seems beyond belief that Paul would write so impersonal a letter to a Church with whom he had closer personal connections than any other.

2. The early Church fathers did not have the word *Ephesus* in the address. Origen has it that the letter is addressed 'to the saints who *are* and who are faithful'. He explains this by saying that those who *are* are the people who share the life of the God whose name is *I am;* they really are; they have the secret of real being, of real life, of the life of God. So Origen thinks that the letter was written to those who possess the life of God, and who are faithful to their trust.

3. The strongest and the best reason for thinking that the word Ephesus is not original is that it is not in the oldest and the best Greek manuscripts of the letter. What then is the explanation of all this?

There is one explanation which does meet the facts. It is very likely that the Letter to the Ephesians was a circular letter meant for all the Churches in the district. That such a letter existed is entirely probable. In the Letter to the Colossians Paul tells the Colossians to read the letter that is on the way to them from Laodicea (Colossians 4: 16). Strangely enough, Marcion knew the Letter to the Ephesians under the title the Letter to the Laodiceans.

It seems very likely that the letter we know as the Letter to the Ephesians was in fact a circular letter which Paul sent to all the Churches of the district. And if that is so, no wonder it is the Queen of the Epistles, for it is uniquely, not a letter to a Church, but the letter to the Church. Originally, then, in the address it would have a blank, to be filled in by Tychicus as he read it to congregation after congregation. We ask one more question—if this is so, how did it come to be known as the Letter to the Ephesians?

The reason for this we can only guess. It is very likely that Paul's letters were first collected and edited in Ephesus. It may well have been that, when the collection was made, and when there was no letter to the Church in Ephesus itself, the Ephesian editors annexed this circular letter, which must have come to Ephesus as one of its destinations, with the idea that a collection of Paul's letters could not go out without a letter to the Church where he had worked so long and which had been so dear to him. In any event we know that the Letter to the Ephesians has a special importance because it began by being sent, not to one, but to many Churches.

What then does this very special letter say? The Letter to the Ephesians has above all to do with the purpose of God in Jesus Christ. That purpose was to unite all things in him, things in heaven and things on earth (1: 9, 10). The universe was meant to be a unity, but instead of the picture of unity, it presents the spectacle of universal division. Man is torn in two between the flesh and the spirit, the higher nature and the lower nature. Mankind are torn in two with Jew and Gentile divided in hatred rather than united in love. Man and God are divided, because man in self-willed rebellion has gone his own way, and has refused both the commands and the love of God. Even in heavenly places there is battle between the demons and the devils, and the angels and God. Instead of a united universe we are presented on every side with the picture of fragmentation and disunion. It is God's aim to unite all things in Christ, so that man's disunity may become the unity which God intended for his world.

1. First, man is to be brought into unity with himself. By the grace of God operating through faith, man can be changed, so that the old evil nature dies and the new nature is born (2: 1-10). The war in the soul is won for good, and the victory comes not by the achievement of man but by the grace of God. In Christ man ceases to be a walking civil war, and becomes a new unity.

2. Second, man is brought into unity with man. Gentile and Jew become one in Christ. The dividing wall of hostility is broken down (21: 11-22). In the phrase *the dividing wall* there is a vivid picture. In the Temple the first court was the Court of the Gentiles; into that court any man of any nation might come. But beyond that there were the Court of the Woman, the Court of the Israelites, the Court of the Priests, and the Temple proper with the great altar of the burnt-offering, the altar of incense, the shew-bread and all the holy things. Beyond the Court of the Gentiles the Gentiles could not go. That Court was surrounded by a low wall, and in the wall at intervals there were set stone tablets saying that, if a Gentile passed that dividing wall, the penalty was instant death.

But in Christ the division is gone; there is no longer Jew or Gentile; there is one new man (2: 15). Here in this passage there is what ought to be the essence of ecumenism. There is to be one *new* man; the word for new is *kainos;* and *kainos* does not mean new in point of time; it means new in point of kind and quality. It is not that the Jew became a Gentile or the Gentile a Jew. Both became a new man. It is, says Chrysostom, as if you put into a fire a statue of silver and a statue of lead, and there came out a statue of gold.

To translate this into modern terms—the end of ecumenism should not be that Presbyterians accept bishops and

Episcopalians accept presbyters; it is not to turn the Anglican into Presbyterian or the Presbyterian into an Anglican. It is that out of the two in Christ there should come something new and far more wonderful than either.

Our aim should not be to make others what we are; it should not be to accept what someone else is; our aim ought to be a union in Christ in which we and the other person become together something gloriously new. There is no question of one dominating the other; both must be dominated by Christ.

3. Man is brought into unity with God. He is reconciled to God (2: 16). Yet again a vivid picture is used. Twice it is said that through Jesus Christ we have *access* to God (2: 18; 3: 12). The word *access* is in Greek *prosagoge*. In the ancient world a king was hedged around with protection; he had to be. At court there was an official called the *prosagogeus*, the person who gave *prosagoge*, access to the king. He was able to admit and to debar; he was what we could call the introducer to the presence of the king.

Jesus Christ is our introducer to the presence of God. By his cross and by his sacrifice (2: 13, 16) the way is open to God. The breach is healed.

4. We have now to take another vast step. God's aim is to produce this new unity in a divided world, and God's instrument is Jesus Christ. But Jesus Christ is no longer here in the body, though he is in the Spirit, and therefore he too needs an instrument, and *his instrument is the Church*. So we have the tremendous thought—God's instrument is Christ; Christ's instrument is the Church. And this is the meaning of the Church as the body of Christ. The Church has to be a voice, a mind, hands, feet to bring into the world that unity which is the dream of God.

'The Church,' says Paul, 'which is his body, the fulness of him who fills all in all' (1: 22, 23). The word *fulness* is the word *pleroma. Pleroma* has two meanings, It means *that which is filled;* so the Church is that which is filled by Christ. But it also means *that which fills or completes.* It is, for example, used of the crew of a boat or the filling of a cup; so the Church is that which fills up Christ, the complement of Christ, the instrument and agent without which Christ cannot do his work. If Jesus Christ, for example, wants a child taught or a land evangelised, he has to find a person to do it for him. That is why the Church is the body of Christ. He is the head who directs and controls it (1: 22), but it is the body through which he acts (1: 23).

So, then, in the Letter to the Ephesians we are given as nowhere else the function of the Church. It is God's purpose that the world should be a unity; his instrument to produce that unity is Jesus Christ. It is Jesus Christ's work to create this unity; his instrument is the Church—and that is why the Church's greatest title is the Body of Christ.

Questions for discussion

1. How within a parish can a congregation genuinely be the body of Christ?

2. If the aim of Christ is to produce one new *man,* if it is not a question of one Church accepting the structure of another, but of the production of something totally new, what do you think might be the structure and the pattern of the one united Church of the future?

3. How can we combine looking back and valuing our history, and looking forward and under God working out something new for the future?

4. Do you think that there should be a change in the message of the Church as well as in the structure of the Church? Or, if there is not to be a change in the message of the Church should there be a change in the form and the method in which it is presented?

5. How do you explain the tragic fact that the Church, which is meant to be the instrument of unity, has so often been the instrument of disunity?

Further reading
Commentaries by William Barclay (*Daily Study Bible*), E. F. Scott (*Moffatt*, in one volume with Colossians and Philemon), George Johnston (*New Century Bible*, in one volume with Philippians, Colossians and Philemon), John A. Allan (*Torch*), F. Foulkes (*Tyndale*).

11 · The letter of joy

The Letter of Paul to the Philippians

When Paul wrote his Letter to the Philippians, he was in prison in Rome (1: 7, 12-14), awaiting trial. The letter had a double occasion. It was to thank the Philippians for the gift which they had sent to him (4: 14-18). But it was to do more than that. The bearer of the gift of the Philippians had been Epaphroditus. But in Rome Epaphroditus had fallen ill. He was both sick for home and worried because he knew that his Philippian friends had heard that he was ill, and he knew that they were bound to be worried about him. So Paul was sending home Epaphroditus, with a warm tribute to the man who had risked his life for the sake of Paul and the Gospel (2: 25-29).

Philippi, to which the letter was written, was a very important town. It took its name from Philip, king of Macedonia and father of Alexander the Great, who had founded it about 350 B.C. There was more than one reason for Philippi's importance. It stood on the edge of a vast plain, watered by the river Gangites, which is a tributary of the Strymon, and that plain was one of the most fertile areas in the world. Long before Philip had founded Philippi, a place called Krenides, which means the Springs, had stood there. Further, Philippi had been the centre of both gold and silver mining. By New Testament times the mines were exhausted, but Philip had been able to work them, and, as one historian said, the gold and silver of Krenides opened more gates to Philip than all his artillery did, for often bribery will buy an entry when force cannot achieve one.

But the greatest reason for the importance of Philippi was its geographical position. There is a mountain range which almost continuously separates Europe and Asia, but at Philippi that range dips into a pass. So, then, Philippi was the gateway between two continents, and that is precisely why Philip made the new city out of the old settlement.

The Romans had tied their vast empire together with a series of great roads, and one of the greatest of these roads, the Via Egnatia, the Egnatian Road from Dyrrachium to Constantinople, passed through that dip in the mountains which Philippi commanded. It was for this reason that at Philippi there was fought one of the great decisive battles of the world, the battle at which Brutus and Cassius, the last defenders of the Roman Republic, were defeated by Mark Antony and Octavian, who, as Augustus Caesar, was to become the first of the Emperors. It was at Philippi that the ancient Roman Republic died and the new Roman Empire was born. All this left its mark on Paul's dealings with Philippi.

So important was Philippi that in B.C. 42 Augustus made it a Roman colony. A Roman colony was not like a modern colony, a piece of newly discovered and freshly explored and annexed territory. The Roman colonies were strategic road centres, the military key centres of the Empire, the vital centres on which the safety and the unity of the Empire depended. To man them, there was sent out a detachment of veteran Roman soldiers, who had served their time in the army, and who had been rewarded with the citizenship. Colonies were miniature Romes. Their inhabitants had a pride in their city which had no parallel. The veterans marched out to them under their own standards. They had their own coinage. Their dress, their speech, their law was Roman. Colonies were, if possible, more

Roman than Rome, with an immense pride in their city and in the Empire which they represented.

We can hear the pride breathing through their first charge against Paul and his friends: 'These men advocate customs which it is not lawful for us Romans to accept or practise' (Acts 16: 21). 'Us Romans'—there speaks the Roman pride. And their respect for Roman citizenship is shown by the speed with which they climbed down when they discovered that Paul was a Roman citizen (Acts 16: 35-40).

All this comes out in the letter. 'Only let your manner of life be worthy of the Gospel of Christ' (1: 27). *Your manner of life* is a verb, *politeuesthai; politeuesthai* is the verb from the noun *polites*, which means a *citizen*; so *politeuesthai* means *to behave as a citizen.* Paul is saying to them: 'You know what citizenship means. You are citizens not only of Rome. You are citizens of the Kingdom of Jesus Christ. Act always in accordance with that citizenship.' 'You are proud of your Roman citizenship,' he says. 'Be prouder still of your citizenship in the Empire of Jesus Christ.' 'Our commonwealth is in heaven, Paul writes (3: 20).

The NEB has: 'We are citizens of heaven.' Here is the same thing again. 'You are citizens of Rome,' Paul says, 'and you are proud of it. You are something far greater—you are citizens of heaven.' The idea of citizenship was dear to the Philippians, and Paul used it to appeal to them as citizens of Christ.

We read of what actually happened to Paul in Philippi in Acts 16. The nature and the character of Philippi explain the events of that chapter. Remember, Philippi was the gateway between Europe and Asia. In Acts 16 in Philippi three people are brought into the Christian Church.

First, there is Lydia. She was a dealer in purple, and therefore a merchant princess. The purple dye came from a little shellfish called the *murex*, one drop from each shellfish. It cost literally hundreds of pounds per pint. She came from Thyatira, from Asia. She was in the very top bracket of society, in the millionaire class.

Second, there was the little fortune-telling slave girl, the ventriloquist by natural gift, the 'belly-speaker' as both the Greek and English words mean. When she spoke it was supposed to be the voice of a god, and her masters were making a fortune out of her. She came from the other end of the social scale, a waif and a stray, a little Greek Macedonian slave, a little penniless piece of flotsam in the sea of ancient society.

Third, there was the Philippian gaoler. He was a Roman official, one of that sturdy, respectable, dependable middle class, who formed the civil service of Rome, and who ran the Empire.

Lydia—the Asiatic—the merchant princess—from the highest stratum of society; the little slave-girl—the Greek—the waif and stray—from the lowest possible level of the social scale; the gaoler—a Roman—respectable middle class—the backbone of the Empire. Asiatic, Greek, Roman; top brass, outcast, middle class; wealthy, penniless, respectably salaried— they are all there in Philippi, *and they are all there in the Christian Church.*

Thus early there was in the Christian Church a cross section of society, a cross section of nationality, from the top to the bottom of the social scale, from the east to the west of the world. Philippi shows us the ideal of the Christian Church in miniature.

In the Letter to the Philippians there are certain key ideas, certain notes which are struck and struck again.

1. The Letter to the Philippians is *the letter of joy*. Again and again the words *joy* and *rejoice* occur (1: 4; 1: 18, 19; 3: 1; 4: 1; 4: 4). It is written by a man who is old and tired with tramping the world for Christ. It is written by a man in prison, with death in all probability not far away. And yet the

beginning, the middle and the end are joy. In the Fourth Gospel one of the great promises of Jesus is: 'No one will take your joy from you' (John 16: 22); and the Letter to the Philippians is the proof that that is true. In Christ there is a joy which no tribulation can darken and a freedom that no prison can take away.

2. The Letter to the Philippians is *the letter of the two worlds*. One of Paul's repeated appeals is that the day of Christ is coming (1: 9-11; 2: 16; 3: 20, 21). The New Testament is full of men and women who are waiting. The length of time they will wait is not the point. The point is that the Christian is a man who is for ever living between 'the already and the not yet', between 'the here and now and the there and then'. And just because of that the Christian is a man who sees all things in the light of eternity, and whose one aim is to be ready for the call of his Lord.

3. For that very reason, the Letter to the Philippians is *the letter of progress*. It is in this letter that Paul likens himself to the man who on the race-track is pressing for ever onwards towards the goal. 'Forward!' is the watchword of the letter. Lord Moran, Churchill's doctor, once heard Stalin quote a Russian proverb: 'A man's eyes should be torn out, if he can only see the past.' The Christian, as Paul in this letter sees it, is a man who forgets the things that are behind and presses on to the things that lie ahead.

4. The Letter to the Philippians is *the letter of sufficiency*. 'I have learned,' says Paul, 'in whatever state I am, to be content.' As the NEB has it: 'I have learned to find resources in myself, whatever my circumstances.' The word which Paul uses is *autarkes*. This was one of the great Stoic words, the very basis of the Stoic creed. It describes the person who is entirely self-sufficient, who cannot be moved or affected by anything outside himself.

The Stoic's aim was to teach himself not to care. Begin with a broken cup, says Epictetus; go on to a torn robe; to the death of a pet animal; teach yourself to say: 'I don't care', and in the end you will be able to stand by and see your dearest die, and say unmoved and self-sufficient: 'I don't care.' Everything, said the Stoic, of joy or sorrow, of laughter or tears, of sorrow or of pleasure, is the will of God anyway. So, when it comes, accept it and say: 'I don't care.' In other words, you can make yourself self-sufficient by killing love. The Stoics, said T. R. Glover, made a desert in the heart and called it a peace. Paul, too, was self-sufficient, but his sufficiency came from him who strengthened him in all things (4: 11-13). The Stoic aimed at absolute independence; the Christian aims at absolute dependence—on Christ.

5. Lastly, the Letter to the Philippians is *the letter of the humble heart*. Philippians 2: 1-11 is one of the supreme passages of the New Testament. It tells how Jesus Christ in his humility emptied himself of his glory and became a man and a servant, and was obedient to death, even the death of the Cross; and out of this humility there came to him the supreme glory. There is little doubt that Philippians 2: 1-11 is an early Christian hymn, a hymn in which the deepest things were put into poetry for the heart to sing what the mind cannot understand. Perhaps Paul wrote the hymn; perhaps he quotes what some unknown poet wrote before him. But the summons to us is to have a like humility that we may have a like glory.

Joy, the sense of the two worlds, the life that is ever on the way, the sufficiency which comes from utter dependence on Jesus Christ, the utter humility whose only greatness lies in service—these are the notes of the Letter to the Philippians—and they are the notes of the Christian life.

Questions for discussion

1. The early Church was an all-inclusive Church, with people in it from the top to the bottom of the social scale. The modern Church tends to be a respectable middle-class institution. Why the difference? Can we get back the inclusiveness? Does this situation differ in a small town or village and in a city?

2. What does it mean to live (a) as a good citizen of our country? (b) as a good citizen of the Kingdom of Christ?

3. How can we maintain Christian joy? What would you say to a depressed, gloomy, tense, pessimistic, irritable, nervous Christian? Or, are you rather like that yourself?

4. Do Christians tend to live in the past? What will it mean in practical action to forget the things behind and to reach out to the things in front?

Further reading
Commentaries by William Barclay (*Daily Study Bible*), R. P. Martin (*Tyndale*), George Johnston (*New Century Bible*), F. W. Beare (*A. and C. Black*), H. G. G. Herklots (*The Epistle of Paul to the Philippians: A Devotional Commentary*).

12 · The all-sufficient Christ

The Letter of Paul to the Colossians

The strange thing about the Letter to the Colossians is that it is one of the greatest letters Paul ever wrote, and yet, as Lightfoot says, it was written 'to the least important church to which any epistle of Paul is addressed'. As Moffatt put it, it is a significant deliverance to an insignificant church.

Colosse was one of three towns which stood close to each other in the valley of the River Lycus, about a hundred miles from Ephesus. Two of them, Laodicea and Hierapolis, stood on opposite sides of the Lycus, six miles apart and in full view of each other. Colosse was twelve miles farther up and straddled the river, which cut the town in two.

Laodicea became famous as the centre of the provincial government; it was a Roman assize town; it was there that Cicero held his court when he was proconsul. It was the centre of the banking arrangements of the province and a very wealthy town. Hierapolis—the Sacred City the name means—was well supplied with hot mineral springs, and became a famous spa. Colosse was a rather insignificant market town, and today there is not even a stone to show where once it stood.

Colosse and the whole neighbourhood had two famous characteristics. The neighbourhood was a volcanic area, and life could be dangerous. Again, the waters of the River Lycus itself and of the tributaries which flowed into it were impregnated with chalk, and the chalk solidified and built up the 'most fantastic grottoes and cascades and archways of stone'. Strabo the ancient geographer has the odd bit of information that 'the water of the springs so easily congeals and changes into stone that people conduct streams of it through ditches, and thus make stone fences'. The local conditions gave Colosse its two great industries. Volcanic ground is fertile ground, and in the magnificent pasture land sheep grazed, from the fleece of which a cloth was made that was world-famous. And the waters were specially suitable for dyeing, for which Colosse was so well known that a certain famous purple dye was called after it.

The area in which Colosse stood had a large Jewish population. Away back in 197 B.C. Antiochus the Third had taken two thousand Jewish families from Babylon and Mesopotamia and had settled them with special privileges in Phrygia and Lydia. Their numbers may be seen from the fact that in 62 B.C. Flaccus the governor prohibited the export of currency, which kept the Jews from legally sending the Temple tax to Jerusalem. The Jews attempted to send it illegally, and twenty pounds weight of solid gold was seized, which would represent the contributions of some 11,000 people. Women and children were exempt from the tax, and no doubt much of it got through, which means that there must have been perhaps as many as 50,000 Jews in the area.

Colosse was not a church which Paul had founded or had ever even visited. The Colossians are included among those who had never seen his face (2: 1). It was largely a Gentile church, for at one time it was estranged and hostile (1: 21), but now it knew the wealth of the mercy of God to the Gentiles. No doubt it had been founded during Paul's two years in Ephesus when all Asia heard the word of God (Acts 19: 10), and it is probable that the founder of the church was Epaphras, who was minister of the church when Paul wrote his letter to it (1: 7; 4: 12). It was Epaphras who had brought news to Paul (1: 7, 8). Much of the news was good. Paul is glad to know of their faith in Christ and their love for men, and of the good order and the firmness of their faith (1: 4, 8; 2: 5). But there is the threat of trouble.

There were three things which would be a danger in any Gentile congregation in New Testament times.

1. There was astrology. The ancient world lived under the tyranny of the stars. Long ago the Babylonian astrologers had marked the unvarying order of the stars; there was an atmosphere of predestination about it all. The next step was to regard the stars and planets as personal gods. The next step was to endow them with power over men, and to believe that a man's destiny was unalterably fixed and settled according to the star under which he was born. Men believed in the iron determinism of a fate fixed by and in the stars. So the trade in horoscopes was widespread. If a man was going on a journey, planning a marriage, laying a foundation stone, he would have his horoscope cast; and it would cost him as much as five pounds, in those days a very considerable sum.

The astrologers prospered and prospered dangerously, for one of the things people tried to find out through astrology was when some rich relative would die, and when a date was given, there was every temptation to make it come true. The ancient world was haunted by astrology. It is against this astrology that Paul warns when he warns the Colossians against belief in the elemental spirits of the universe (2: 8, 20). The man who believes in the power of Christ cannot still believe in the power of the stars.

2. There was syncretism. It was an age when men accepted a kind of amalgam of religions. The Roman Emperor Alexander Severus had in his private chapel images of Abraham, Orpheus, Apollonius and Christ. Maximus of Tyre said that any man of

sense believed in one supreme God; but ignorant men can only make their guesses about him. So, 'God is a name which all religions share'. Symmachus said in a speech in the Roman senate: 'There cannot be one way to so great a secret.'

But Christianity will have none of this. There is in Christianity what Bultmann calls a divine intolerance. This is why Colossians has its tremendous Christology. Jesus Christ is the image of the invisible God: in him all the fulness of God is pleased to dwell (1: 15-20). In him are hid all the treasures of wisdom and knowledge (2: 3). In him the fulness of deity dwells in a body (2: 9, 10). Christ is all-sufficient; nothing and no one else is needed. In a syncretistic world the Christians insisted on the unique Christ.

3. There was Gnosticism. Gnosticism was the supreme enemy of Christianity. It was a way of thought rather than a special church or school or heresy. The Gnostics tried to explain the existence of sin and evil, and they did so like this. Matter and God, they said, are co-eternal. Matter has always been there from all eternity. Out of this already existing matter the world was made. But this already existing eternal matter was flawed; it was bad stuff. Since this is so, the true God could not create, because he could not touch this soiled matter. So he sent out an emanation and this emanation sent out another emanation and so on and on. Each emanation was further from God; each emanation was more ignorant of God; at the end of the long line there is an emanation who is distant from God, ignorant of God and hostile to God; that is the god who created the world. This has extreme and terrible consequences. It means that the creator of the world is the enemy of God. Christianity retorted with the belief that it was through the Son, through Christ that all was created, and that therefore creation is of God (1: 16, 17).

If Gnosticism is true, then Jesus could not have had a body;

he could not have taken matter upon him; he was no more than a phantom, a ghost with no body. Christianity insists that in him the fulness of God dwells in a body (2: 9, 10). The Gnostics held that to involve God in the material affairs of life is to dishonour God; Christianity holds that God so loves the world that in Jesus Christ he came bodily into it. Gnosticism has moral and ethical consequences. Two things can happen.

A man can believe that since matter is bad, the body is bad and that therefore a man must live in rigid asceticism, denying the body everything it may want. Such a man will practise ritual observance in food and days and seasons (2: 16, 17). Such Gnostics are always saying: 'Don't touch this; don't taste that; don't handle the next thing.' 'Do not handle, do not taste, do not touch,' is the Gnostic, not the Christian watchword (2: 21-23). A man who has given his life to Christ should be long past rules and regulations (2: 20). Strangely enough, the ascetic Gnostics often accepted and practised the Jewish law.

On the other hand, a man may say, 'Since the body is evil, it does not matter what I do with it. I will state and glut its desires. It makes no difference.' But to the grosser sins the Christian should be dead (3: 5-8). There is in Christianity a death, a life and a hope. The Christian died with Christ and died to the old life of sin (3: 3). The Christian rose with Christ and lives life in the Lord and in his life (3: 17, 18). Christ will come, and to that hope the Christian moves (3: 4). The Christian has no use for asceticism, and less use for self-indulgence. The Christian enjoys life lived in Christ.

Gnosticism has a last consequence. A man's soul is a spark of God in him; that spark has to get back to God. To get back it has to climb the ladder past all the emanations, right back to God. To do that, so the Gnostic says, it needs all kinds of passwords and all kinds of esoteric knowledge. The conclusion is clear. Salvation is only for the intellectual elite, for the chosen few, the ordinary man can never attain it. But again Christianity will have none of this. As Paul says: 'Him we proclaim, warning *every* man and teaching *every* man in all wisdom, that we may present *every* man mature in Christ' (1: 28). The thrice repeated 'every man' is the hammer-blow against the exclusiveness of the Gnostics.

Astrology, syncretism, Gnosticism—these were the great dangers of the time, and the Letter to the Colossians deals with them magnificently in the light of Christ.

Questions for discussion

1. How do you think a Christian should react to astrology, fortune-telling and the like? Do you think that there is no harm in it, or do you think there is a certain danger in all this, even when it is not taken seriously? Do you think that even people who say they do not take it seriously sometimes have a lurking feeling that there is something in it?

2. What are you going to say to people who argue that there is good in all religions? The Gnostic would have agreed that Jesus is the highest of the emanations, but would still have said that he was only one of many. What would you say to this?

3. What is the place of asceticism in the Christian life? Must a Christian, for instance, be a total abstainer? Think what the Jewish saying means: 'A man in the judgment will have to give account for every good thing he might have enjoyed and did not enjoy.' Can the Christian ethic really be expressed in listing things we may not eat or drink or do?

Further reading

Commentaries by William Barclay (*Daily Study Bible*), H. M. Carson (*Tyndale*), F. C. Synge (*Torch*), George Johnston (*New Century Bible*), William Barclay (*The All-Sufficient Christ*).

13 · The importance of the present

The Letters of Paul to the Thessalonians

The name Thessalonica does not raise the same memories and pictures as the names of Athens, Corinth or Rome do. But in the ministry of Paul, his coming to Thessalonica was of epoch-making importance. Thessalonica was in Macedonia, and so was Philippi; and when Paul was writing to Philippi years later he described his coming to Macedonia as 'the beginning of the gospel' (Philippians 4: 15). When the gospel came to Macedonia, to Philippi, to Thessalonica, it was as if it had made a completely new beginning.

There is drama in Luke's story, told with such economy of words, of how the gospel came to Macedonia (Acts 16: 6-10). It is a story of door after door shutting until at last God's door opened. They wanted to preach in Asia, but the Holy Spirit forbade them. They tried to preach in Bithynia, but the Holy Spirit would not allow them. And so they came to the sea-coast at Troas. And there, as they waited for the Spirit's guidance, there came the vision of the appeal from Macedonia, and in answer to it Paul and his friends set sail.

This is one of the epoch-making journeys to the world—for by that voyage the gospel came to Europe. That was why the coming to Macedonia could be called 'the beginning of the gospel', for in that mission Christianity made a new beginning. It began the campaign for Europe; it set out on the task of being not the religion of any continent, but the religion of the world.

81

So Paul landed at Neapolis—and the gospel had come to Europe (Acts 16: 11), and from there he went to Philippi (Acts 16: 12-40). Thence Paul came by way of Amphipolis and Apollonia to Thessalonica (Acts 17: 1). Thessalonica was a city of 70,000 inhabitants, of whom as many as 20,000 were Jews. The supreme importance of Thessalonica lay in this: the Roman Empire was bound together by a series of great roads. One of the greatest was the Egnatian Way, which went from the Adriatic to the Hellespont; from Rome to Byzantium. The main street of Thessalonica was actually part of that road. Thessalonica was 269 miles from the Adriatic and 265 miles from the Hellespont. Plant Christianity in Thessalonica and it could travel west until it reached Rome and east till it reached Byzantium. Here indeed was a new beginning for Christian mission.

Paul preached with power and many were won for Christianity, especially among the Greeks, who in their search for a purer and higher religion had attached themselves to the Synagogue. But the Jews stirred up a riot; Paul and his company were charged with being revolutionaries, hostile to Rome, and Paul and Silas had to escape by night to Beroea (Acts 17: 1-10). And if we read that passage carefully, the clear implication is that the whole business happened in a brief three weeks (Acts 17: 2).

The Jews made trouble in Beroea too, and Paul was smuggled out by ship to Athens (Acts 17: 10-15); and from there he went on to Corinth (Acts 18: 1). Paul was desperately worried about what was happening in Thessalonica, so he sent Timothy to find out (1 Thessalonians 3: 1, 2) and out of Timothy's report there came the Letters.

There were certain things that were making Paul very anxious.

1. There was one thing which must have been behind his

whole thinking. He had been in Thessalonica for only three weeks. Was it possible to make a mark on a place in three weeks? If it was, then there was hope that the gospel might spread like a flame through Europe. But if it was going to be necessary to settle down in a place and to work for months and years before there was any effect, then the outlook was grim. The supreme question was—could a community of Christians grow up in three weeks? This was what was worrying Paul—but he need not have worried. It has always been true that Christianity is caught rather than taught, and the saving and the changing power of the gospel made it spread like a contagion wherever it went.

2. Clearly, there was also a threat to the character of Paul (1 Thessalonians 2: 1-12). We can read between the lines, and we can see that Paul was being accused of using deceitful and guileful seduction; that he was accused of pleasing men with flattery; and he was accused of greedily using the gospel as an excuse for feathering his own nest; that he was accused of being dominating and dictatorial. There is one charge about which Paul was very sensitive, the charge of using his mission for his own profit and his own glory. 'You remember our labour and toil, brethren; we worked night and day, that we might not burden any of you, while we preached to you the gospel of God' (1.2: 9). 'We were not idle when we were with you; we did not eat anyone's bread without paying, but with toil and labour we worked night and day, that we might not burden any of you' (2.3: 7, 8). The day was to come fifty years later when the wandering prophet and apostle who made use of the hospitality of congregations in order to live soft became one of the scandals of the Church.

The first book of order and discipline which the Church ever produced was called the *Didache: The Teaching of the Twelve Apostles*, and there it is laid down that a wandering evangelist may stay one day or two days in a community, but if he stays for three days, he is a false prophet. If he asks for money, or for a table to be spread for him, he is a false prophet (*Didache* 11, 12). The Church has always had its spongers. The important thing is this—Paul was not concerned with his own prestige or his own glory, but Paul knew quite well that the character of the missionary will be the cause of the success or the failure of the mission. He knew that he, like all preachers of the word, must by the grace of God be above suspicion.

3. There was the threat to holiness (1.4: 1-8). The Christian should be on the way to sanctification. The Greek for sanctification is *hagiasmos;* all Greek nouns which end in *-asmos* describe a process; and *hagiasmos* is the road to holiness. The Thessalonians were only one step away from the paganism in which they had been born and in which they had lived: the Christian Church was like a little island of holiness in a sea of immorality; relapse was so easy. We may put it this way—if the Christian is not going forward, he is going back. For him life should be the continual onward march towards sanctification, towards holiness.

4. There was the threat to fellowship (1.4: 9, 10; 1.5: 14, 15). They already love; but they are to love even more. Nor is their love to stop at Thessalonica; it was to go out, and it did go out, all over Macedonia. It is worth noting that Christian love is a stunted and truncated thing when it does not see beyond the congregation, and there are many Christians who love their congregation without loving the Church. Further, this love is to be the kind of love which encourages the faint-hearted and helps the weak and is patient with all. Christian love is not a sentimental but a curative love.

5. There was the threat to authority (1.5: 12, 13; 2.3: 14, 15). The Thessalonians are urged to respect and to obey their leaders and to take heed to what Paul is saying. It is as well to

remember that democracy has never meant the right to do what one likes but rather the obligation to act together for the common good.

6. There is the threat to worship (1.5: 19-22). Inspiration is not to be stifled; prophetic utterances are not to be despised; everything is to be tested and the good is to be kept and the bad is to be avoided. Even at that early time the Thessalonians were having to face the problem of how to combine the spontaneous and the formal in the worship of the Church, how in the services of the Church to link together individual freedom and that order which makes communal worship possible.

7. But the main problem in the Church at Thessalonica was a misunderstanding for the Second Coming. The Second Coming had been preached to them, and their whole idea of Christianity was dominated by it. They had left their idols to wait for the coming of God's Son from heaven (1.1: 10). The motive which kept them in purity and chastity was that they might be found without fault when their Lord came (1.3: 13; 1.5: 23). The Thessalonians will be Paul's own hope and joy and crown at the coming of their Lord and his (1.2: 19). Although there were to be signs of it (2.2: 1-12), it was to be as sudden and unexpected as a thief in the night, and that very fact was the motive for chastity and sobriety, so that, whenever Jesus Christ came, he would find them ready (1.5: 1-8). They fully expected it in their own life-time for Paul can speak of 'we who are left to the coming of the Lord' (1.4: 15). There were two problems.

(a) The Thessalonians were worried about those who had died before the Lord came. Would they lose their share in the coming glory? Paul reassures them that at the coming of the Lord those who have died and these who are still alive will be caught up to meet the Lord (1.4: 13-18). We have to remember when we read this passage that it comes from a time when Christians expected the Second Coming at any moment, and when they took their pictures of it from scenery which they had inherited from the Judaism from which they came.

(b) But there was a more serious problem than that. This concentration on the Second Coming had at least for some in Thessalonica disrupted the ordinary activities of life. They had abandoned work; they did nothing but stand about watching the sky and talking in excited groups. They had thus become the laughing-stock of the community, and they had become a burden to the Christian Church, for they had ceased to make any attempt to earn their living (1.4: 11, 12; 2.3: 6-13). Paul's command is that they should go quietly and calmly about their business, earning their living and being a burden to no man, for there is something badly wrong with the Christianity, or rather the alleged Christianity, which turns a man into an hysterical, excited, idle busybody. It is Paul's conviction that when Jesus does come, the best possible way we can be found is conscientiously doing the day's work, earning our living in purity, and serving our fellowmen in charity. A man's Christianity should make him a better, not a worse, workman.

As Moffatt says of these two letters: 'Every paragraph of them runs out into the future.' Of course, the Christian has a future, but he cannot prepare for it better than by remembering the importance of today.

Questions for discussion

1. Discuss the importance of the lives of professing Christians in the missionary work of the Church at home and abroad. What are the things in professing Christians which can repel those who are outside the Church?

2. Discuss the relationship of the individual to the community, whether in the state or in the Church. How far

have we the right to insist on following out our own ideas?

3. Paul worked with his hands as a tent-maker. Every Jewish Rabbi had to have a trade by which he earned his living. Do you think it would be a good thing for a Christian minister to have an 'ordinary' job as well as his ministry?

4. It has been said of the Second Coming that, either Christians never think of it at all or they never think of anything else. Is this true? What is the place of the doctrine of Second Coming today?

Further reading
Commentaries by William Barclay (*Daily Study Bible*), William Neil (*Moffatt* and *Torch*), Leon Morris (*Tyndale*), A. L. Moore (*New Century Bible*).

14 · Slave and brother

The Letter of Paul to Philemon

The Letter to Philemon is unique among the letters of Paul, because it is the only personal letter that Paul wrote which we possess. No doubt Paul wrote many personal notes, and no doubt these notes shared the fate of most personal letters—they were read and immediately destroyed. Before we are finished of our study of this letter, it may be that we shall find out why this scrap of personal correspondence was preserved, and why it got into the New Testament at all.

There are two views of this letter. One of them is simple and straightforward; the other is much more speculative and imaginative and romantic. We shall begin with the simpler of the two views.

The letter to Philemon is about a runaway slave called Onesimus. It is likely enough that he was a thief as well as a runaway, for Paul writes to Philemon, Onesimus' master: 'If he has wronged you at all, or owes you anything, charge that to my account. I Paul write this with my own hand. I will repay it' (18, 19). This runaway had found his way to Rome, just as today an escaper might make for London, hoping to be lost in the crowded streets of the thronging city. Somehow or other Onesimus had made contact with Paul, and through Paul's influence he had become a Christian (10). Paul puns on his name. Onesimus means useful. At last the useless one is true to his name and is now really the useful one (11). But Paul could

not harbour a runaway slave, and Paul is sending Onesimus
back to his master. Paul is under no illusions about the danger
of what he is doing.

Allard writes in his book on slavery in the ancient world: 'It
is in the Roman Empire that we see slavery in all its horror.' A
slave was not a person; he was a thing, or at best an animal.
For the purposes of customs duties slaves were classed with
horses and mules. Ulpian the jurist writes about 'the slave or
any other kind of animal'. Caius another jurist speaks of
'slaves, animals and other things'. The master could do literally
anything to his slave—scourge him, imprison him, mutilate
him, and even kill him. Gaius writes: 'We may note that in all
nations the master in regard to the slave possesses the right of
life and death.' In his book on farming Cato counsels the
economical head of a family 'to sell old oxen, to get rid of
imperfect calves or sheep, wool, skins, old carts, old imple-
ments—and the old and sick slave'. The slave was thrown out
to die.

The numbers were immense. In the reign of Augustus we
read of a man who, even after he had lost his fortune in the
civil wars, still possessed four thousand one hundred and sixty
slaves. Petronius tells us that in one day on Trimalchio's estate
thirty boys and forty girls were born to his slaves. Prices were
high; a good slave could cost as much as £1,000. They were
sold like animals, stripped, made to stand on a pedestal,
pawed, prodded, trotted round like horses. The pettiest faults
brought the most savage punishments. Augustus crucified a
slave for accidentally killing a tame quail; Domitian roasted in
an oven a slave who had made his bath water too hot; Vedius
Pollio flung into the fishpond, to be torn to pieces alive by the
lampreys, a slave who had dropped and broken a crystal
goblet.

A speck of dust, a piece of imperfectly polished silver, the failure to chase a fly away, a table not perfectly set, a chair out of position, a sneeze or a cough or a whispered word while waiting at table, wine served or a bath filled at the wrong temperature, brought out the whip or worse. The mistress tore with her nails or lashed with the leather thong the maid who misplaced a curl, while preparing her for an assignation. If a master was murdered, all his slaves were executed, and in the case of Pedianus Secundus this involved more than four hundred men.

Of course, there were masters who were kind to their slaves. Seneca, believing in the Stoic doctrine of the brotherhood of man, did not hesitate to eat with his slaves. Pliny sent a sick slave to Egypt to recover from an illness and to the farm of a friend to recuperate. He would liberate his slaves before they were too old, and, although a slave had no legal rights, he would regard it as a sacred duty to carry out the slave's dying wishes. There were good masters, but inescapably a slave was a 'thing'.

For a slave to run away was the most serious of crimes. If he was caught he might well be crucified, and certainly he would be branded on the forehead with a red hot iron, marked for life with the letter F, which stood for *fugitivus*, which means runaway. Clearly, Paul was taking a tremendous risk in sending Onesimus back. Paul would have loved to keep Onesimus. To send him back was like tearing out his very heart; but he would do nothing without Philemon's consent (12-14). So Paul implores Philemon to receive Onesimus back as he would have received Paul himself, to receive him back 'no longer as a slave but more than a slave, as a beloved brother' (16). What happened—on this view—we do not know, but it is hard to see how Philemon could have resisted an appeal like that.

Before we go on to look at the view which tries to take the story further, there are certain things we must note.

(a) A great many people have wondered why Paul did not use the opportunity of these happenings to pronounce against slavery and to condemn it as unchristian. There is just this to be said—it may well be that even Paul regarded slavery as a built-in fact of life. There were sixty million slaves in the empire, and life without them was almost inconceivable. And, if Paul had pronounced against slavery, and if the Church had urged the slaves to revolt, at that time the only result would have been a bloody massacre, in which thousands and thousands would have perished. What Christianity did do was to sow a seed which soon or late would make emancipation inevitable.

(b) But Paul takes the sting out of slavery. Onesimus is to go back as a slave, but also as a brother beloved. Maybe it was out of his talks with Onesimus that Paul thought out his instructions both to masters and slaves (Ephesians 6: 5-9; Colossians 3: 22-4: 1), and 1 Timothy 6: 1, 2 shows that there could arise a situation in which a slave used his Christianity to be a disobedient and an inefficient slave, and to think that, because his master was also a Christian, he could get away with it. Paul's advice to slave and master alike is to remember that they both have a master above, and, if men are beloved brothers to each other, it does not matter whether or not you call them master and slave, for there is a new relationship which has made so-called status irrelevant. If master and slave are brothers who love each other, the problem is already solved.

But now let us look at the view which tries to take things further. It is hard to see how Philemon could avoid sending Onesimus back to Paul. Paul writes: 'I would have been glad to keep him with me, in order that he might serve me on your behalf during my imprisonment for the gospel, but I preferred to do nothing without your consent, in order that your goodness might not be by compulsion, but of your own free will' (13, 14). It would be hard to resist that. Suppose then that Onesimus came back to Paul, and helped and learned. It is highly probable that Paul's letters were collected, edited and published in Ephesus round about A.D. 100 or thereby. Not long after A.D. 100, Ignatius the great bishop of Antioch was being taken to Rome to be burned for being a Christian, and, as he went, he sent letters to the Churches of Asia Minor which he had known so well. He wrote to Ephesus and he reminded the people of Ephesus of the excellence of their own bishop: 'A man of inexpressible love and your bishop. I plead with you by Jesus Christ to love him, and to resemble him. For blessed is he who granted to you to be worthy to obtain such a bishop' (Ignatius, Ephesians 1: 3). What is the name of this wonderful bishop? *It is Onesimus.*

Can it be that the runaway slave has become the great bishop of Ephesus? And can it be that the editor of the collection of the letters of Paul was Onesimus? And can it be that Onesimus put into this collection this little letter about himself, as if to say: 'See what I was—a runaway slave, a thief and a criminal! And see what the grace of God has done for me!' It may be so; we hope it is so. And if it is so, then the little letter to Philemon is in the New Testament to bear witness to what Christ did for a man's life and soul.

Questions for discussion

1. What is the essential difference between a slave and a workman?

2. Aristotle always held that there are certain men who are meant by nature to be hewers of wood and drawers of water, who are meant by nature to do the world's menial tasks. Do you agree that there is truth in this? Or do you think that all men are equal? Suppose a man has to spend his life in a very ordinary task, how can he help himself to find satisfaction in it?

3. Do you think that any problem can be faced and tackled at any time, or do you think that the time can be genuinely inopportune, and that we must wait until the right time comes?

4. Do you think that any amount of legislation and any amount of social change can be effective without a change in the attitude of people to each other? How can we teach ourselves to look on the other man as 'a brother beloved'?

Further reading
Commentaries by William Barclay (*Daily Study Bible*), H. M. Carson (*Tyndale*), E. F. Scott (*Moffatt*), George Johnston (*New Century Bible*). John Knox's *Philemon among the Letters of Paul* (Collins) works out the Onesimus story.

15 · The letters of the Church

The Letters of Paul to Timothy and Titus

Nowadays First and Second Timothy and Titus are always referred to as the Pastoral Epistles, but they did not always have that name. The earliest list of New Testament books, the Muratorian Canon (about A.D. 170) regarded them as personal letters, and said that they were written for the sake of affection. It thus distinguished them from the other letters, which were written not to persons but to Churches and communities. But it soon became obvious that these letters were a great deal more than personal letters. Thomas Aquinas (about 1250) said that First Timothy was 'a kind of pastoral rule', and that it handed over to Timothy everything that was necessary for 'the training of bishops'. He said of Second Timothy that it gave 'instructions about ecclesiastical order'. Since they were regarded as having to do with the training of bishops, by the seventeenth century they were being called the pontifical letters.

But in 1726-1727 Paul Anton, in a course of lectures given at Halle, described them as the supreme Pastoral writings, 'the supreme example of writings suitable to those who seek preparation for, and guidance in, the Christian ministry', and from that time on the title Pastoral Epistles stuck to these letters. The letters themselves tell us their own object. They are written that 'you may know how one ought to behave in the household of God, which is the church of the living God' (1 Timothy 3: 15)—and very certainly that is always a lesson worth learning.

It is quite clear that by the time these letters were written the Church was well on the way to being a well organised institution. This means that they are later than the other letters, and that they come from a stage in the history of the Church after them. There are many scholars who think that, as they stand, they do not come from the hand of Paul; such scholars believe that in the later days of the Church, near the end of the first century, in times when the life and faith of the Church were under threat, some one, who possessed some genuine fragments of personal letters that Paul had written, issued these fragments, together with a message for the times in which he lived.

Whatever else is true, it is certain that these letters came out of a developed situation. They contain what may be among the earliest fragments of Christian hymns:

> 'He was manifested in the flesh,
> vindicated in the Spirit,
>   seen by angels,
> preached among the nations,
> believed on in the world,
>   taken up in glory.'
>
> (1 Timothy 3: 16)

> 'If we have died with him,
>   we shall also live with him;
> If we endure,
>   we shall also reign with him;
> If we deny him,
>   he also will deny us;
> If we are faithless,
>   he remains faithful—
>   for he cannot deny himself.'
>
> (2 Timothy 2: 11-13).

They contain what looks like a fragment of one of the earliest creeds:

'Remember Jesus Christ, risen from the dead, descended from David.'

(2 Timothy 2: 8).

There is one of the first references to baptism as the means of regeneration (Titus 3: 5). There are references to the laying on of hands as the way in which the divine gift is transmitted to the young man entering upon the ministry (2 Timothy 1: 6; 1 Timothy 4: 14). Clearly, the Church is becoming an institution with its own worship, its own creeds, and its own liturgy and ceremonial.

But the change in the situation is much more radical than that. The supremely important change is that in these letters we have reached a time when the Church has a public image. The Church is no longer a little private company of followers of Jesus Christ. The Church is an institution and organisation set down in the midst of the world. It is an island in a sea of paganism—but an island that is visible to all. Men and women are coming to it just out of heathenism. Relapse is so desperately easy; the tainting infections are so fiercely strong. It is a fact that to this day missionaries tell us that of all the books in the New Testament the Pastoral Epistles are most relevant to the missionary situation of a young Church.

1. First, these letters deal with the *institution* of the Church. They lay down the regulations for the bishop (1 Timothy 3: 1-7); the elders (Titus 1: 5-9; 1 Timothy 5: 17-19); the deacons (1 Timothy 3: 8-13); the order of widows (1 Timothy 5: 3-16). Both in a Jewish and a Greek community we would expect to find elders. Every Jewish town and village had its elders, who dispensed justice and ruled the synagogue. But in every Greek village, too, we would have found the elders of the fishermen, or the elders of the cultivators, or the elders who were

responsible for the good order of the village. The eldership had a long history on both sides of the Church.

At this stage of the Church it is fairly certain that elder and bishop were different terms for the same office. The qualifications for the elder and the bishop were to all intents and purposes identical (1 Timothy 3: 1-7; Titus 1: 5-9). The word elder describes the man in his person—he was literally an elder, and older man; the word bishop describes him in his function—for the word bishop (*episkopos*) means an overseer or superintendent. Elder describes what the man was; bishop describes what the man did. The work of the elders lay in the teaching and preaching and administering side of the Church. The word deacon (*diakonos*) means a servant, and a servant in practical things, and the deacons carried out the practical work of the Church.

When we look at the qualifications for any of the offices in the Pastoral Epistles (Titus 1: 5-9; 1 Timothy 3: 1-7; 1 Timothy 3: 8-13) certain interesting things emerge. The Church official was first and foremost to be a good, sober, clean-living man. He was to be a good teacher, able to state and to support his case, and to do so with courtesy. He was to be a man who had proved himself, and not someone who had shot to the top of the tree with spectacular speed. He must rule his own family wisely and well, for the man who cannot rule his own family is certainly not fit to rule the Church. And the most interesting regulation of all was that the Church official must be in good standing with those outside the Church as well as with those within it. The point which emerges—and it is of supreme importance—is that the one qualification for office was *character*. The Church did not depend on a *new system*; it depended on *new men*. Whatever else a man had, if he had not character, he was not qualified for the leadership of the Church.

2. Second, these letters deal with the *faith* of the Church. Things were happening to threaten the purity of the faith (1 Timothy 1: 3-7; 2 Timothy 3: 1-9; 4: 3, 4), and the letters provide a defiance. Certain things are very noticeable here. When we talk of *faith*, the word has two meanings. First, it means that living, vital, personal connection between us and Jesus Christ, Second, we can also talk of the faith in the sense of a creed, a body of belief. Faith is either the spirit which believes, or the beliefs which are believed in. In Paul's great letters faith is the personal committal of the soul to Jesus Christ; in the Pastoral Epistles faith tends to mean a body of belief (1 Timothy 4: 1; 4: 6; 6: 10). In the Pastorals faith is not very far from meaning orthodoxy. No one can read the Pastorals without noticing how often the word *sound* appears, sound doctrine, sound teaching, sound speech, people who are sound in the faith (1 Timothy 1: 10; 6: 3; 2 Timothy 1: 13; 4: 3; Titus 1: 9; 1: 13; 2: 1; 2: 8). The stress in the Pastorals is on being orthodox, on maintaining the proven and accepted belief of the Church.

That produces another very significant picture. In the ancient world one of the most sacred of all obligations—perhaps the most sacred—was to return uninjured, unharmed and intact any trust that has been committed to us. The gods looked with grave displeasure on a man who failed in a trust. That is the way in which the Pastorals think of the faith. They think of the faith as something which has been entrusted to us, something which we must preserve in all its pristine purity and splendour, and something which in our turn we must hand down and hand on. The faith is something which we have had the privilege to receive, the duty to preserve, and the obligation to transmit. It is not unfair to say that the Pastorals are more concerned with the preservation of the faith as it is than with the adventure of the development of the faith into new vistas and new discoveries, but the Pastorals were undoubtedly providing for the needs of their day.

3. Out of all the wealth of the teaching of the Pastorals we can only select two more things. The Pastorals have two important things to say about the Church. First, the Church is to be a praying Church (1 Timothy 2: 1.2, 8). And second, the Church is to be a Bible-reading Church. The Pastorals believe that to seek God's presence and to listen to God's word are primary essentials.

4. The Pastorals are always sensitive to the image that the Church is presenting to the world, and they have two things to say of the Christian in the world. First, they insist that the Christian must be a good citizen, praying always for those who have the responsibility of government (1 Timothy 2: 1.2), and living a law-abiding and useful life (Titus 2: 1.2). It is in the world that the Christian must demonstrate his Christianity. Second, they insist that the Christian must do an honest day's work, that he must never think that a Christian employed by a Christian master can use their mutual relationship as an excuse for getting away with less than his best (1 Timothy 6: 1.2).

There are many other things in the Pastorals, but three things stand out—the conviction that character is the best equipment for the office-bearer in the Church; the belief that the best defence against false teaching is the presentation of that truth which the Church has inherited and must transmit; the certainty that the best propaganda for Christianity is a Christian life lived in an unchristian world.

Questions for discussion

1. Given the right character, what further technical and theological equipment ought the Church office-bearer to have?

2. How can we preserve both the unchangeableness and the

adaptability, both the fixity and the flexibility of Christian doctrine?

3. What part do you think Christians should play in the world of industrial relationships?

4. Do you think that the Church can still be said to be in the middle of a Christian society, or do you think that the situation of the Church today resembles that of the Church of the Pastorals, and that it is now again in the middle of a pagan society?

Further reading

Commentaries by William Barclay (*Daily Study Bible*), D. Guthrie (*Tyndale*), E. F. Scott (*Moffatt*), E. F. Brown (*Westminster*, from the missionary point of view), J. N. S. Alexander (*Torch*), J. N. D. Kelly (*A. and C. Black*).

16 · Let us draw near

The Letter to the Hebrews

To those to whom the Letter to the Hebrews is one of the supreme books of the New Testament, the fact that it was one of the latest books to establish its right to be part of Scripture at all must come as a shock. The trouble was that no one ever knew, and no one knows, who wrote the Letter to the Hebrews. The catechetical school at Alexandria was the great centre of scholarship in the early Church. There, about the year A.D. 200, Pantaenus possessed the Letter to the Hebrews, but noted that it had come to him without any author's name. About A.D. 215 Clement of Alexandria thought that it might be the work of Luke. About A.D. 250 Origen, the greatest scholar of them all, delivered his famous verdict: 'Who wrote the Letter to the Hebrews God only knows for certain.'

In Caesarea, Eusebius, the untiring investigator of Scripture, writing about A.D. 340, had to class the Letter among the disputed books; it was neither altogether accepted nor altogether rejected; it was in a state of suspense. In the East the place of Hebrews was settled by the Easter Letter of Athanasius written in A.D. 367. In an age when heresy was rampant Athanasius wrote telling his people the books which the Church accepted as Scripture, and the Letter to the Hebrews was one of them. In the West the story was the same. In the Muratorian Canon, the first official list of the books of the New Testament, which the Church at Rome drew up, Hebrews does not appear

101

at all. Tertullian thought that it might be the work of Barnabas. In the West the balance was tipped by Jerome, the man to whom we owe the Latin Bible, the Vulgate. He did not know who wrote the Letter. 'Whoever it is who wrote the Letter to the Hebrews,' he writes. But he did include it.

The trouble was that the test for any book as part of the New Testament was: Is it the work of an apostle, or is it the work of an apostolic man, that is, a man who had been in personal touch with Jesus and the first apostles? That is why at first the Letter to the Hebrews was not considered as part of Scripture, and that is why in the end it was attributed to Paul. It was known; it was loved; it was valued. None could gainsay its greatness. The only way to ensure its place in the New Testament was to include it with the Letters of Paul, and so that was done. It may well be said that the Letter to the Hebrews forced its way into the New Testament. Calvin wrote: 'Let us not allow the Church of God or ourselves to be bereft of so great a blessing. . . . We need however feel little anxiety as to who wrote it. . . . I cannot myself be brought to believe that Paul was the author. . . . The method of instruction and style show that the writer was not Paul.' As a modern writer said: 'We cannot tell whose hand actually penned the Letter to the Hebrews, but we can be sure that the Holy Spirit wrote it.' The Letter to the Hebrews got into the New Testament, because it could not be kept out.

Suggestions have been made as to its authorship. As we have seen, Tertullian thought that Barnabas wrote it, and Barnabas was a Levite who would know all about the temple worship of which the Letter is so full (Acts 4: 36). Again we have seen that Clement of Alexandria thought that Luke might have written it, because the Greek is rather like the Greek of Acts. Two modern suggestions are interesting. Harnack thought that Aquila and Priscilla wrote it between them, and that it has no author's name because a woman wrote it, and in those early days that was a thing a woman was forbidden to do. Luther thought that perhaps Apollos wrote it. Apollos was from Alexandria, the place of scholars; he was an eloquent man and mighty in the Scriptures (Acts 18: 24); and that is certainly the kind of man who wrote the letter.

What then is the Letter to the Hebrews all about? The ancient world was haunted by the thought of the complete transcendence, the utter distance of God. God was indeed in Otto's famous phrase *The Wholly Other*. Maximus of Tyre said of God: 'The Deity himself is unseen by sight, unspoken by the voice, untouched by fleshly touch, unheard by hearing.' Plotinus described God as 'abiding still and beyond all things'.

It is the same in the Old Testament. God is so different that he is dangerous. Moses hears God say: 'You cannot see my face; for man shall not see me and live' (Exodus 33: 20). When Manoah and his wife realised who their visitor had been, Manoah says in terror: 'We shall surely die, for we have seen God' (Judges 13: 22). No one could enter the Holy of Holies except the High Priest, and he only on the Day of Atonement, and at no other time 'lest he die' (Leviticus 16: 2). How could man ever find access to a God like that?

But there was another aspect of this in Greek thought. Plato had worked out his famous conception of forms or ideas. In the heavenly places there are ideal forms of which everything on earth is a pale and imperfect copy. For instance, to take it at its simplest, there is in heaven the perfect form, the perfect idea of a chair of which all earthly chairs are poor and imperfect copies. As Plato said in the *Timaeus:* 'The Creator of the world had designed and carried out his work according to an eternal and unchangeable pattern of which the world is but a copy.' Ideas, said Seneca, 'are what all visible things were created from, and what formed the pattern of all things.' 'We have no real and life-like likeness of real law and genuine justice; all that we enjoy is a shadow and a sketch,' Cicero said. We can put this in another way in more modern language. Here we have imperfect copies; somewhere there is the invisible world of *reality*. How are we to get from the shadows to reality?

The Greeks and the Hebrews were really asking the same question. The Hebrew asked, 'How do we find access to God?' The Greek asked, 'How do we find access to reality?' And the triumphant answer of the writer to the Hebrews is, 'You have access to God and access to reality in Jesus Christ.' This is the basic thought of the Letter to the Hebrews. In Jesus Christ we have access to the true tabernacle which God pitched, not men (8: 2). In him we reach the things that cannot be shaken (12: 27). In him we reach the city whose maker and builder is God (11: 10). In him we have a better hope by which we can draw near to God (7: 19). The whole letter is written on the one text: 'Let us draw near' (10: 22). Jesus Christ is the way to reality and to God.

So then the writer to the Hebrews sets out to establish from every angle the lonely supremacy of Jesus Christ.

1. Jesus is greater than the prophets (1: 1-3). The revelation which came by the prophets was spasmodic and fragmentary. Jesus is the agent of creation; he is the purifier of men; he is the Son in whom the very likeness of God is perfectly seen.

2. Jesus is greater than the angels (1: 4-2: 9). The angels may be called the sons of God, but no angel is ever called the Son; no angel is worshipped; the final victory is the victory of Jesus Christ, even if that victory is won through suffering and death.

3. Jesus is greater than Moses (3: 1-6). He is greater in the way in which the architect and the builder of the house is greater than the house itself; he is greater in the way of which a son is greater than a servant.

4. Jesus is greater than the Old Testament Aaronic priest-hood. The priest in Latin is *pontifex*, which means a bridge-builder; the priest is the person who builds a bridge between man and God; he ought to be the person in whom the longed-for access is found. There are certain essentials of a priest. A priest must be like the people he represents, sharing their nature, knowing their temptations; Jesus is truly like men (2: 17; 4: 14-16; 5: 2). A priest does not take the work of priesthood to himself; he must be called by God to it, and Jesus is truly called (5: 4-6). The main function of a priest is to offer these sacrifices which will open the way to God (5: 1; 8: 3). But Jesus differed radically from all earthly priests.

The earthly priest has to begin by offering sacrifices for his own sin before he sacrifices for the people (5: 3; 7: 27). This is something that Jesus never needs to do. The sacrifices of the earthly priest are obviously in one sense unavailing, for they have to be offered day in and day out, over and over again (9: 25; 7: 27; 10: 1, 2, 11). There is no end to them. But the sacrifice Jesus Christ makes is made once and for all and never needs to be made again (9: 12, 26: 28; 10: 10, 12, 14). The sacrifice which the earthly priest makes is an animal sacrifice and is unavailing to ease the wounded conscience (9: 9, 13; 10: 3, 4); the sacrifice which Jesus made is the sacrifice of himself, and of his own perfect obedience to God (9: 16; 10: 5, 10), and that is the only truly availing sacrifice. He is the new priest after the order of Melchizedek (chapter 7).

All that Jesus has done has introduced a new relationship between God and man. That is to say Jesus is the bringer of a new covenant, that covenant of which Jeremiah wrote, in which God's law is written not in books but on the heart, in which the need of sacrifice is gone, in which God remembers sin no more (Jeremiah 31: 31-34; Hebrews 8: 8-12; 10: 16, 17). In connection with this three great words are used of Jesus.

1. He is *archegos* (2: 10; 12: 2), the pioneer. The *archegos* was the founder of a new city, the bringer of a new teaching, the man who blazed the trail; the pioneer is the one who goes first for others to follow.

2. He is the *prodromos* (6: 20). The *prodromos* was the reconnaisance man who went first to make it safe for others to follow, the pilot who guided the ship into the safety of the harbour, the forerunner. So these two words describe Jesus as the one who has opened the way to God for others to follow.

3. He is the *mesites*, the mediator (9: 15; 12: 24). The *mesites* is literally the man who stands in the middle. Jesus stands in the middle between man and God, bringing God to men and men to God.

To the writer to the Hebrews, Jesus is supremely the one who for us opens the way to God and to reality. 'Let us then with confidence draw near to the throne of grace, that we may receive mercy and find grace to help in time of need' (4: 16).

Questions for discussion

1. Do you find it worrying that we do not know who wrote the Letter to the Hebrews, or do you agree that the human writer does not matter, if it is the work of the Spirit, no matter who wrote it?

2. Of all the New Testament Letters, Hebrews needs most study. The tabernacle and its furnishings, the ritual of the Day of Atonement (Leviticus 16), the covenant idea, the Platonic conception of reality—to understand Hebrews we need to know something about them all. Does this seem to you to put Hebrews at a disadvantage in the twentieth century?

3. What do we really mean by access to God?

4. Note how the Letter to the Hebrews holds the balance between Jesus as the divine Son of God, and Jesus the truly

human person. Do we always succeed in maintaining that balance, or do we sometimes over-stress the divine and sometimes the human? Which side of Jesus are we in most danger of overstressing?

Further reading
Hebrews is especially rich in study material. See commentaries by William Barclay (*Daily Study Bible*), H. W. Montefiore (*A. and C. Black*), T. Hewitt (*Tyndale*), T. H. Robinson (*Moffatt*), E. C. Wickman (*Westminster*), F. V. D. Narborough (*Clarendon Bible*), W. Neil (*Torch*), William Barclay (*Lutterworth Bible Guides*), A. B. Bruce, E. F. Scott, J. P. Alexander (*A Priest for Ever*).

17 · Practical Christianity

The Letter of James

The Letter of James had a hard struggle to get into the New Testament. In the Latin-speaking Church, in the Muratorian Canon, (the first official list of Christian books, dating to about A.D. 170), the Letter of James does not appear at all. Tertullian, who flourished about A.D. 200, has no fewer than 7,258 quotations from the New Testament, and not one of them from James. The earliest Latin manuscript of James dates to A.D. 350. It was not until Jerome included James in the Vulgate that the place of James was safe. In the Syriac, and Syriac would be the language of Palestine, there was not so much as a translation of James until A.D. 412. In the Greek Church both Origen and Eusebius had their doubts about James, and it is not until the famous Easter Letter of Athanasius in A.D. 367 that James finds a place in Greek scripture. In the modern Church this Letter has always suffered from the fact that Luther disliked it so much, because it seemed to set too much stress on works and too little on faith. 'A right strawy epistle,' Luther called it. 'I do not hold it,' he said, 'to be of apostolic authorship.'

And yet the strange thing is that of all New Testament books there is none so immediately relevant today. There is hardly a sentence of James which is not completely intelligible to the modern man.

We can never be quite so sure who the James was who wrote it. Tradition identifies him with James the brother of Jesus; but one would have thought that a letter written by the brother of our Lord would have had no difficulty in establishing its place in scripture. It starts as a letter, and it could not claim to have a wider public, for it claims to be written to all the Jews scattered throughout the whole wide world. But it does not finish as a letter; it has no final greetings and no final farewell. But it is possible to make a fairly certain deduction as to what this letter originally was. No one has ever succeeded in making a coherent plan of the contents of James. It flits from subject to subject, throwing out pearls of wisdom, each of them unconnected with what goes before or follows after. The Jews had their own theories of preaching. One of their main beliefs was that the preacher, in order to maintain the interest of his hearers, must never linger for long on any one subject; he must keep moving quickly and constantly from one subject to another. They called preaching *charaz*, which means stringing pearls; and that is exactly what James is—a handful of pearls dropped one after another into the mind of the hearer. There is little doubt that this Letter began life as a Synagogue sermon. One of the things that turned Luther against it is that there is so little in James that is distinctively Christian. There are only two references to Jesus (1: 1; 2: 1); there is nothing about the Cross, the Resurrection, the Holy Spirit. There was no more Jewish figure in the Church than James the brother of Jesus; and it is very likely that this is one of his Synagogue sermons which someone took down and published. Let us then pick up some of the pearls which James scatters.

1. It is James' conviction that trial is meant to produce character (1: 2-4). Trial produces *steadfastness*, which in Greek is *hupomone*. *Hupomone* was far more than the patience which sits down and endures. It was the Greek word for 'a masculine constancy under trial'. It is the Christ-given ability to turn tragedy into triumph, always to see the glory beyond the

gloom, always to be able to trace the rainbow through the rain.

2. It forbids a man to put the blame on God for his temptations and for his fall (1: 13-15). The Jews believed in the doctrine of the two natures, which teaches that in every man there are two natures, a good nature beckoning him up, and an evil nature dragging him down. Where did the evil nature come from? Some said that man developed it himself; some said it was the result of Adam's sin; some said Satan put it there. But the common belief was that, since God created everything, he created the evil nature too. So the Rabbis could make God say: 'It repents me that I created the evil tendency in man; for, if I had not done so, he would not have rebelled against me.' 'I created the evil nature for you; I created the Law as an anti-septic!' They therefore found it possible to blame God for their own sin. We still do. Remember Burns:

> 'Thou knowest thou hast formed me
>   With passions wild and strong;
> And listening to their witching voice
>   Has often led me wrong.'

There are many who have said, and say: 'I can't help the way I'm made'—which is equivalent to putting the blame for our sin on to God.

3. James condemns with violence snobbery in the Church (2: 1-7). It was hard for the humble people of the early Church not to regard a man of wealth or birth or status as someone deserving special treatment. In the presence of God there is no such thing as status; for in the presence of God every man, whatever his fortune or his social rank, is nothing more than a hell-deserving sinner.

4. James is intensely aware of the danger of wealth (1: 10; 5: 1-6). At its best wealth is something that vanishes away. At

its worst wealth is a crime, when it is withheld from those who have earned it by a master who is more concerned with wealth than justice.

5. For James, religion is the most intensely practical thing. Real religion is to visit the fatherless and the widow and to live a clean life (1: 27). When Donald Soper was asked the usual question at the beginning of his ministry, if he had a passion for souls, he answered that he was not quite sure what a soul was. But he had a great love for people. Concern is the first characteristic of the Christian. James did not see that there was any use in expressing a pious wish that some cold, hungry person should be warmed and fed, without doing something to see that he was (2: 15, 16). The man who brings back one sinner from the wrong way will not only save another, but will also find salvation for himself (5: 19, 20). James is always asking, 'What have you done to turn emotion into action?'

6. James believed that in the world there are two kinds of wisdom (3: 13-17). There is the wisdom which makes a man worldly wise and the wisdom which makes a man heavenly minded. The curse of life is covetous ambition; and the blessing of life is the clean heart and the humble mind (4: 1-10). Not to put too fine a point upon it, we can be wise unto salvation and wise unto damnation.

7. There are two things with which the name of James will always be connected. The first is the terror of the tongue (1: 26; 3: 1-12). The tongue as James saw it is one of the most dangerous forces in the world. There are few more damnable sins than the sin of gossip; and the murder of some one's good name in the tittle-tattle over the tea-cups is something God is not going to forget.

8. And above all, there is James' insistence that faith without works is dead (2: 14-26). An immediate question arises. Is James at variance with Paul? In Paul a man is

justified by faith; no man is justified by works of the law. There are three things to be said.

(a) When Paul talks about works of the law, he means washing of hands, observance of the trivialities of the Sabbath law, circumcision, food laws and the like. When James talks about works, he means love and justice and kindness and generosity and concern. Paul would have completely agreed that the Christian faith must produce the Christian life.

(b) There are two kinds of belief. There is intellectual belief which is merely a thing of the mind; there is moral belief which dominates life. I believe that the square on the hypotenuse of a right-angled triangle equals the sum of the squares on the other two sides—but it makes no difference to me. I believe that five and five make ten; I will therefore refuse to pay twelve pence for two five pence articles. The one belief left my action untouched; the other directs it. Paul would thoroughly have agreed that intellectual acceptance of a dogma is of no use in itself; faith is not Christian faith unless it issues in Christian action.

(c) Paul and James are talking of different stages in the Christian life. In the first step of the Christian life a man is saved by faith alone. He cannot earn the love and the grace of God; he can only take in the faith that what Jesus says and shows about God is true. But once a man has accepted Christ, then life must be one long effort to be worthy of that love which loved me and gave itself for me, and to walk in the footsteps of that Christ who walked to the Cross for me. To put it very shortly—a man is not saved *by* works; but he is saved *for* works, and his faith is not faith unless it begins by accepting and goes on to living.

Questions for discussion

1. Does snobbery still exist in the modern Church?
2. Do we ever blame God for our faults? Do we ever say:

'I can't help it. That's the way I'm made'? Do we really believe that the grace of Jesus Christ means that no man need stay the way he is?

3. When does the possession of money become a crime? When do ways of making money become a sin?

4. Is it really enough to say that true religion consists in visiting the fatherless and the widow and keeping ourselves unstained from the world? What about worship, the sacraments, study of the Bible, real belief, prayer?

Further reading
Commentaries by William Barclay (*Daily Study Bible*), C. L. Mitton, J. Moffatt (*Moffatt*, in the volume on the General Epistles), R. V. G. Tasker (*Tyndale*), E. C. Blackman (*Torch*), R. J. Knowling (*Westminster*), E. Sidebottom (*New Century Bible*, in the volume on James, Jude and 2 Peter).

18 · The obligations of grace

The First Letter of Peter

It has been said that of all the New Testament letters the First Letter of Peter is the easiest for a modern man to read. Izaak Walton used a quartet of adjectives to describe the General Epistles of James, John and Peter—'affectionate, loving, lowly, humble'—and this description is specially applicable to this Letter of Peter. It has been said that the distinctive characteristic of Peter's Letter is *warmth*. Moffatt said that it has two aims, steadily to encourage 'endurance in conduct and innocence in character'.

It is quite possible that the First Letter of Peter consists of two addresses interwoven into one. A doxology naturally comes at the end, and 4: 11 ends with a doxology. So it is suggested that 1: 3 to 4: 11 was originally a baptismal sermon—3: 21 talks about baptism—and that it was meant to underline and outline the duties of people who had newly been baptised into the membership of the Christian Church. The following passage, 4: 12 to 5: 11, has then been taken to be another sermon addressed to the Church when persecution was threatening, and when life was in jeopardy, urging Christians to be steadfast in their loyalty and their faith. Be that as it may, it is true that this Letter is a clarion call to duty in difficult circumstances.

Peter begins with the basic conviction that the Christian is a man reborn (1: 3; 1: 23). Something has happened to the

114

Christian which has meant so radical a new beginning in his life that it can only be compared to being born all over again; there is a complete break with the past and a complete new beginning as a new person. This new beginning, this rebirth puts a man into a whole series of relationships.

1. The Christian is in a relationship to Jesus Christ. It has often been argued that Peter has what is called an *exemplarist* Christology, that is, that he sees the work of Jesus Christ as the morally moving power of a great example, a power so effective that the new example makes a new man. He has left us an example that we should follow in his steps (2: 21). The word for *example* is in Greek *hupogrammos*, which is the word for the line of perfect copperplate handwriting at the top of the page of a child's writing exercise book; and just as the child learns to write by copying the perfect writing pattern, so, it is said, the Christian learns to live by copying the perfect pattern of life in Jesus.

As we shall see, there is much more than example in Peter's view of Jesus. What there is in Peter is a passionate sense of obligation. He never mentions what God or Jesus has done for us without pressing on us the obligation which this action for us brings. It is for obedience that we are chosen, destined and sanctified (1: 2). It is not with silver and gold that we have been ransomed, but by the blood of Jesus Christ, the lamb without blemish and without spot. *Therefore* we must be obedient children (1: 13-21). We have experienced the supreme kindness of the Lord. *Therefore* put away all evil things (2: 1-3). We have received the mercy of God. *Therefore* live like a holy people (2: 9, 10). Christ suffered for us. *Therefore* leave the sins of the past behind (4: 1-6). The end is near. *Therefore* live in that love which befits those who are stewards of the grace of God (4: 7-11).

Again and again Peter presses on the Christian the utter

obligation that the mercy of God and the suffering love of Christ lay on the Christian. Clement of Rome spoke of 'the yoke of grace'. Peter's insistence is that no man who has experienced the grace of God and the love of Jesus Christ can remain the way he is. But Peter goes far beyond that in his thought of Jesus. He uses three pictures of Jesus which contain far more than the demanding power of a great example or a great gift.

(a) He sees Jesus as the Passover Lamb (1: 19), for the Passover Lamb was without spot or blemish (Exodus 12: 5); and it was the blood of the Passover Lamb, smeared on the doorpost of the house, which protected that house from the angel of death. The blood of Christ rescues from the death of sin.

(b) He sees Jesus as the suffering servant (2: 21-24). As it has been put, this is Isaiah 53 read by someone who has seen Jesus Christ suffer and die. The servant died for others; so did Jesus Christ.

(c) He sees Jesus as the scape-goat. In the ritual of the Day of Atonement the scape-goat, the goat for Azazel, went out into the wilderness bearing upon it the sins of the people (Leviticus 16-20-22); and so Jesus bore our sins to or on the Cross (2: 24).

It is true that there is in Peter a strong ethical emphasis. Bigg points out that there are two kinds of temperament—the disciplinarian and the mystic. The disciplinarian hears God's voice from without, speaks of Jesus as Saviour, Friend, Master, Rewarder, distinguishes sharply between the human and the divine. The mystic feels the presence of God within, says, 'Not I live, but Christ lives in me', desires to sink his personality in the divine, until he and God are one. Paul is the mystic; Peter is the disciplinarian. It is a matter of temperament, not of faith.

2. The Christian is in a relationship to the world.

(a) If in the *family* one partner is a Christian and the other is not, the life of the Christian partner must be a sermon, silent, but so powerful that it is irresistible. Those who do not obey the word are to be won without a word, by the power of a life (3: 1-6).

(b) In his *day's work* the Christian is to live with a service like the service of Jesus Christ, even if he is cruelly and unjustly treated. As a servant the Christian must reproduce the service of Jesus (2: 18-25).

(c) As a *citizen* the Christian is to live with such excellence that his life will give the lie to all who make charges against him (2: 11, 12; 13-17). Peter is quite sure that there is no argument for Christianity like the argument of a Christian life. The best defence of Christianity is Christian living; the only propaganda for Christianity is the Christian.

3. At the back of First Peter there is the continuous threat of persecution; those who will read this letter are in continual jeopardy of their lives (1: 6, 7; 2: 12, 15; 3: 13-17; 4: 12-19; 5: 9, 10). In face of this Peter insists on certain things.

(a) The purpose of persecution is to produce a faith that is like gold tried in the fire, a faith so purged and strengthened that nothing can break it (1: 6, 7) Persecution is meant to make a man, not to break him.

(b) When charges are made, the only way to disprove these charges is to live in such a way that they are demonstrated to be untrue (2: 12). The Christian defence lies not in words but in life.

(c) It is inevitable that a Christian will have to suffer. Let him see to it that he suffers always for the right, and never as an evil-doer (3: 13-17). Peter would have agreed with Plato that it is better to suffer wrong than to do wrong.

(d) After the cross there comes the crown; after the suffering there comes the reward (4: 12-19). To be reproached for the name of Christ is to have the spirit of glory resting on us (4: 14).

God will be in no man's debt, and at the end of the day the new world will redress the balance of the old.

(e) To suffer for Christ makes us one with that heroic band who throughout the ages and throughout the world have put fidelity before safety, obedience before comfort, and loyalty before life (5: 9). First Peter turns suffering into glory, if the suffering is for Christ.

From First Peter there comes the scriptural warrant for the sentence in the creed which says of Jesus, 'He descended into Hell' (3: 18-20; 4: 6). This is hinted at in other places in the New Testament, along with the final triumph of Jesus in every corner of the universe (Acts 2: 24-32; Romans 10: 6-8; Ephesians 4: 8-10; John 5: 25; Philippians 2: 10; Revelation 5: 13).

We must first note that descended into *Hell* is not the correct translation; it is descended into *Hades,* and Hades was not Hell; it was the place of the dead, to which, it was believed, all the dead went, before any real doctrine of immortality and life after death had emerged. So what Peter says, and what the creed ought to say, is that Jesus descended into the world of the dead. What does this doctrine mean?

(a) It is a natural outcome of wondering what Jesus was doing in the time between his death and his resurrection. Even then he was engaged in his saving work.

(b) It is the statement that there is no limit to the area in which the grace of God can work. Often we ask, What is to happen to those who died before Jesus came, who never had the opportunity in life to hear the Gospel? This doctrine lays it down that they did get the chance, because, it says, in the period between his death and his rising again Jesus took the message of the Gospel to the dead.

(c) It may be that the main aim of this doctrine is to say that Jesus really and truly did experience death; he did really and truly descend into the place of the dead. Jesus did not go through some trance-like sleep; he truly died.

There are only five chapters in First Peter, but it is one of the richest letters in the New Testament.

Questions for discussion

1. What would be wrong with a doctrine which saw in Jesus only the supreme example?

2. How in a modern, industrial society can a man or a woman make his or her life a sermon for Christianity and propaganda for the Christian faith?

3. In what ways can a Christian still be persecuted even in a so-called Christian country?

4. Examine yourselves, and find out whether you are a disciplinarian or a mystic in temperament.

Further reading
Commentaries by William Barclay (*Daily Study Bible*), C. E. B. Cranfield (*Torch*), Ernest Best (*New Century Bible*), A. M. Stibbs (*Tyndale*), A. M. Hunter (*The Interpreter's Bible*), J. Moffatt (*Moffatt*, in the volume on the General Epistles).

19 · Threats to the Church

*The Second Letter of Peter and the
Letter of Jude*

It is almost certainly true to say that Second Peter and Jude are
the least read books in the New Testament. They had difficulty
in establishing themselves in the New Testament at all. When
Origen made his investigation of the standing of the various
books of the Church, he classed them both among the books
which were disputed. Eusebius did the same in the first half of
the fourth century. Eusebius says that no one had any doubts
about Peter's first letter, but that there were many who held
that Second Peter was not part of the canon, although they
read it with interest and with profit.

Calvin had his doubts. From the style of the Greek of the
letter, he did not believe that Peter could have written it,
because it was so different from the first letter. But he held it to
be so valuable and its contents so excellent that it could not be
discarded. He suggested that it was written by a disciple of
Peter, at Peter's request and under Peter's direction. Luther
would have dropped Jude altogether, ·because it was only a
repetition of Second Peter. It does seem very unlikely that First
and Second Peter were written by the same person. But we may
well leave all these questions, saying as Whittingham said in
his New Testament, which was the forerunner of the great
Geneva Bible, that 'seeing the Spirit of God is the author
thereof, it diminishes nothing the authority, although we know
not with what pen he wrote it'. Second Peter and Jude have to

be taken together, because the second chapter of Second Peter to all intents and purposes simply takes over Jude.

The Church was in danger when these letters were written. Jude had been about to write a treatise on the faith, but in the circumstances he laid that undertaking aside to write a defence of the faith (Jude: 3). There are times when a trumpet blast is better than a subtle argument of an exposition of theology. Both writers stress the fact that they are not telling their people anything new; they were reminding them of what they already know (2 Peter 1: 12; 3: 1, 2; Jude: 5). Far oftener than not that with which we need to be confronted is not new truth, but truth which we have forgotten or which consciously or unconsciously we are evading. It is not with novelties but with the things which cannot be shaken that the preacher and teacher must confront his people.

Second Peter begins by reminding its readers that, if they are not to be so blind that they cannot see the truth, so short-sighted that they cannot see their goal, so forgetful that they have forgotten that they have been cleansed, they must carry out an exercise in Christian addition (2 Peter 1: 3-11). They must begin with faith, and faith is absolute commitment to Jesus Christ. To their faith they must add virtue (*arete*). In this sense virtue means the particular quality which a thing ought essentially to have. The virtue of a blade is sharpness; the virtue of a field is fertility. So to the commitment of heart the Christian must add the action of the distinctively Christian life. To attain that life the Christian must add knowledge to his virtue. He must live intelligently, knowing both why he does a thing and how it is to be done. To his knowledge he must add self-control, for only he who is master of himself can ever be the servant of others. To his self-control he must add steadfast-ness (*hupomone*). Sometimes this word is translated patience or endurance, but it is not a passive word at all. It does not describe the patience which sits down and uncomplainingly allows the floodtide of events to flow over it. It has been described as 'a masculine constancy under trial'. It is the spirit which can make a triumph out of a tragedy, and out of sorrow a source of greater joy. To the steadfastness he must add godliness (*eusebeia*). The word means reverence; it is as if to say that the Christian must make the whole of life one continuous act of worship of God. He must be as conscious of God in his work and in his pleasure as at his prayers or in his church. To the godliness he must add brotherly affection. His piety must be such that it unites him to men in fellowship, and does not separate him from them. And to his brotherly affection he must add love. His heart must reach out beyond the family, the group, the congregation so that, like his Master, he lives in love to all men.

Such is the Christian life which is demanded. But the evil men who are a threat to the Church are also described.

1. They are apt to take Scripture and to twist it into meaning what they want it to mean. They must learn that no prophecy is a matter of one's own interpretation (2 Peter 1 : 20). They must read Scripture under the guidance of the Holy Spirit and of the Church.

2. They deny their Master, that master who paid so dearly for them, and they must end in disaster (2 Peter 2: 1). They are Christians who have lost the loyalty without which no man has any right to claim the name of Christian.

3. They are so licentious that they have got their Christianity a bad name (2 Peter 2: 2); in their lust they even pollute the Christian Love Feast, the *Agape* (Jude: 12). The Love Feast was the common meal which Christians ate together on the Lord's Day, each bringing what he could, and sometimes the poor slave bringing nothing but himself and his hunger. The feast which should have been the feast of pure love had become the opportunity for lust.

4. Their greed is such that they will even exploit their membership of the Church for gain (2 Peter 2: 3). They have brought their essential selfishness even into the Christian fellowship.

5. They are more like beasts than men (2 Peter 2: 13-22; Jude: 10-16). They have allowed the animal part of their nature to dominate them, and it would be better for a man not to start out on the Christian way than to start and then to return to the filth he has left (2 Peter 2: 22).

6. They scoff at Christian belief. Because the end is slow in coming they think that it will never come, forgetting that it is only in his mercy that God delays, and that the Christian ought to use the time remaining to prepare for the coming of his Lord (2 Peter 3: 3-15; Jude: 10).

But the pointing finger of history points them to their doom. All history proves, as Froude said, that it is well with the good and evil for the wicked. The wicked angels were destroyed. The flood annihilated evil men. Sodom and Gomorrah came to their dreadful end. But God by rescuing Lot gave proof that he will not fail the man who is true to him (2 Peter 2: 4-10; Jude: 5-7). No doubt is left that evil men are on the way to destruction.

Before we try to identify more closely the evil men, we must note one thing about these two letters which did much to delay their acceptance as Scripture. They both quote non-biblical books apparently as Scripture. 2 Peter talks about the evil angels (2 Peter 2: 4). These are the angels who came to earth and seduced mortal maids (Genesis 6: 1-4) and their story is told much more fully in the Book of Enoch, and it is to Enoch that the reference is. This same book of Enoch is actually quoted in Jude: 14. Further, Jude: 9 speaks about the argument that the angel Michael had with the Devil about who was to get the body of Moses after Moses died. That story is taken from another intertestamental Jewish book, The Book of the

Assumption of Moses. Jerome, for instance, was very doubtful about 2 Peter and Jude because they quoted as Scripture books which were not in the Bible. But these books were very popular and much read when these letters were written, and they were simply taking their illustrations from books which everyone knew.

Finally, let us ask who the evil men were whom these letters castigate so severely. They were antinomians. Antinomians are people who hold that with Jesus Christ the law has come to an end and that there remains nothing but grace. They hold that there is nothing that they cannot do and nothing that they cannot take. At their furthest development they held that a man had a right to take everything he wanted from any shop or any house, and that to take it was not theft; and that a man had a right to any woman, and it was not fornication or adultery. They held that for the Christian there was no such thing as law. Jude sums them up, 'ungodly persons who pervert the grace of God' (Jude: 4). They argued that Christian freedom gave them the right to do absolutely as they liked, and that free grace had, so to speak, abolished sin. There has hardly been a generation in which men like that did not appear within the Church.

They forgot that they were bought with a great price. They forgot the obligation that love lays on any man. They forgot that any man who has been loved as the Christian has been loved is never again free to please himself, least of all to please his lower nature. They forgot that Jesus Christ saved and rescued us, not that we might be free to sin, but that we might be free from sin, free to live to him, and to become pure as he is pure.

Questions for discussion

1. Now that you have read these two letters, do you really get much out of them? Do you think that perhaps they were fortunate to be included in the New Testament?

2. How can we keep in their proper proportions law and grace, freedom and discipline, love and severity, the patience and the wrath of God?

3. Heine said of God: 'God will forgive. It is his trade.' (*C'est son metier*). What would you say to someone who said that to you?

4. Examine yourself in the light of the ladder of Christian virtues in 2 Peter 1: 5-7.

Further reading
Commentaries by William Barclay (*Daily Study Bible*, in the volumes on The Letters of John and Jude and The Letters of James and Peter), J. Moffatt (*Moffatt*, in the volume on the General Epistles), C. E. B. Cranfield (*Torch*, in the volume on 1 and 2 Peter and Jude), E. M. Sidebottom (*New Century Bible*, in the volume on James, Jude and 2 Peter).

20 · The tests of faith and life

The First Letter of John

The First Letter of John was written because it had to be. There was a threat to the faith and the life of the Church, and that threat had to be met, or the consequences would have been disastrous. That threat came from a line of thought that we have met before; it came from Gnosticism. Gnosticism was an attempt to explain the sin, the suffering and the evil of the world. It began with the assumption that all matter is totally and essentially evil, and that spirit alone is good. It further laid down that matter and spirit are both eternal, that both were there from the beginning and before the beginning. It was out of this evil matter that the world was made, and therefore from the beginning the world was made out of bad stuff, out of flawed material.

This basic assumption had another consequence. If matter is altogether bad and if God, who is spirit, is altogether good, it follows that God could not have touched and handled and worked with matter. Therefore, the true God is not the creator of the world. What happened was that God put out a series of aeons or emanations. Each emanation was a little farther from him, and each emanation was a little more ignorant of him. Finally the long line came to an emanation who was infinitely distant from God, who was utterly ignorant of God, and who was completely hostile to God, and that distant, ignorant, hostile emanation was the creator of the world. Often the

Gnostics identified this inferior creating God with the God of the Old Testament, and, they said, the true God, the God who is spirit, is the God of Jesus Christ, the God of the New Testament.

This whole way of thinking had certain results. It meant that the world was bad, because all matter is bad, and that in particular the body is bad. If the body is bad, there can be no such thing as the incarnation. God in Jesus could never have taken a body upon himself. Therefore, so the Gnostics argued, Jesus never came in the flesh; he was only a phantom creature with no real body. That is why John insists that the true Christian must confess that Jesus Christ has come *in the flesh*, that he is a real man, with a real flesh and blood body (4: 2).

Further, if the body is essentially evil, it may well be argued that it does not matter what is done with it. It cannot be made worse anyhow. Therefore a man can be as fleshly and as immoral as he likes. That is why John insists that the Christian cannot say that he has fellowship with God, and then walk in darkness (1: 6).

The word Gnostic means an intellectual, one who claims knowledge. The Gnostic claimed that the soul of man is a spark of spirit which has become imprisoned in the prison house of the evil body. The soul must be told this; it will then wish to escape; and to escape it must learn all the passwords and the knowledge which will take it past all the emanations on the long upward trail to God. That is only for the intellectual; the simple Christian can never rise to knowledge like this. Therefore fellowship is interrupted and people are divided into those intellectually capable of real religion and those too simple for it. And that is why John stresses over and over again the need of love fellowship, between the brethren.

Gnosticism was destroying the incarnation, destroying morality and destroying fellowship, and it was to meet that situation that this letter was written. First of all, the letter has four great things to say about God.

1. *God is light, and in him is no darkness at all* (1: 5). Light, as Robert Law says, is the most beautiful and blessed thing in the world. It is the function of light to be seen; it is the function of light to enlighten. Light is a double emblem; it is the emblem of knowledge and of purity.

So, to say that God is light means that God wants to be known; his self revelation is a necessity of his being. He is not distant and unknown and unknowable. The Christian God is not, as the Gnostics said, the unspeakable silence or the impenetrable abyss. God is the God who reveals himself to his children in Jesus Christ. But, further, in both Greek and Hebrew and in the eastern faiths, light stands for goodness and purity, and darkness stands for evil and corruption. That is to say, God is the source of moral illumination. No religion which comes from God could teach or encourage a man to be impure and dissolute and corrupt. If God is light, then God is the God who makes himself known, and who makes himself known in goodness and in purity.

2. *God is righteousness* (2: 29). Righteousness, as Law says, is 'all that is right in character and conduct'. This whole letter is filled with 'an impassioned sense of the tremendous imperative of righteousness', and 'a rigorous intolerance of sin'. The Christian must first and foremost be a good man (2: 4; 3: 8-10; 5: 18). John is quite clear that God's man does not sin, and that, if a man does sin, he is the devil's man.

3. *God is love* (4: 8). Law calls this the profoundest, gladdest, most transforming truth the mind can conceive'. Love is the attitude of God to men, and must be the attitude of men to God and to one another. This love is the atitutde which is to 'turn all men into brothers'.

4. *God is life* (5: 20). God is the source of life and the giver

of eternal life. Eternal life is not simply life which lasts for ever. It is easy to see that there are circumstances in which long life would be an agony and not a blessing. Eternal life is not life of a certain extent, but life of a certain quality; it is the life of God himself. God's man shares God's life.

But the most interesting thing about this letter is the series of tests of Christianity which it supplies. One of its favourite phrases is, 'By this you know . . .', 'By this we may be sure . . .' (2: 3, 5; 3: 10; 3: 16; 3: 24; 5: 2).

1. There is the test of obedience (2: 3-6; 3: 10; 5: 2). John is very blunt. The man who claims to know God, and who disobeys God's commandments is a liar. Whoever does not do right is not of God. Obedience is the proof of love, and, where there is no obedience, there is no true love.

2. There is the test of willingness to listen to the truth (4: 5, 6). The man who listens to Christian truth is of God; the man who refuses to listen is not. This letter draws a sharp distinction between the Christian and the world. (2: 15-17; 3: 1, 13; 4: 5, 6; 5: 4, 5; 5: 19).

The whole world is in the power of the evil ones, and the Christian cannot expect anything other than misunderstanding and opposition and hatred. John never had any doubt that the Christian is 'different'.

3. There is the test of love (2: 11; 3: 14-18; 4: 7-12). To walk in hate is to walk in darkness. The best proof that we have passed from death to life is that we love the brethren. The love of God must be the pattern of our loving. It is the man who loves who knows God and is born of God. Nor must this love be merely a thing of words or of sentimental emotion. If a man himself is comfortably furnished with this world's goods and sees his brother in need and does nothing about it, God's love is not in him. 'Little children, let us not love in word or speech but in deed and in truth' (3: 17, 18). Emotion must issue in action.

4. There is the test of the possession of the Spirit (3: 24; 4: 13). The possession of the Spirit is not to imply abnormal and ecstatic conduct. The Spirit for the Christian is the atmosphere in which he lives and walks, the power on which he depends to enable him to abide in Christ, the person who is the companion of his way.

5. There is the test of correct belief in Jesus Christ. The Christian must believe that Jesus is the Son of God (4: 15). No human category, however high, is adequate to describe Jesus. It is in terms of divine sonship that he must be regarded. Above all, the Christian must believe in the incarnation; he must believe in the flesh and blood manhood of Jesus; he must believe in the reality of Jesus' full entry into life.

Finally, we may look very briefly at three great facts that this letter lays down about Jesus.

1. Jesus is the advocate with the Father (2: 1). The obligation is on the Christian not to sin, but in this life and in this world perfection is not possible, but, if the Christian does fall, Jesus is there to plead the case of the penitent sinner.

2. Jesus is the expiation for our sins (2: 2; 4: 10). This does not mean that some barrier of God's wrath and anger has to be broken down by some sacrifice of Jesus Christ. It was because God loved us that he sent his Son to be the expiation for our sins (4: 10). But it does mean that the way to God is opened up for us by what Jesus did for us, for can any man who has seen the life and death of Jesus Christ have any doubt left that God loves him?

3. Jesus is Saviour (4: 14). Jesus is sent by God to rescue us from self, and sin, and Satan.

It was a local danger and threat which first produced this letter, but nonetheless it is a letter which has truth for every age and generation—not least for our own.

Questions for discussion

1. One of the tests of the Christian life is obedience to the will of God. How do we learn what the will of God is for us, for life in general and for any particular situation?

2. What will it mean in practical action to regard men as brothers? What will this mean socially, racially, politically, from the point of view of different religions and of different branches of the Church?

3. This letter is insistent that the Christian must not sin. How does this connect up with 'permissiveness'?

4. It is clear that the great danger of the heresy behind this letter was that it threatened to destroy the manhood of Jesus. Whether are we in more danger of losing the manhood or the divinity of Jesus? How can we hold the balance between them? What does it mean to say that Jesus was both God and man?

Further reading
Commentaries by William Barclay (*Daily Study Bible*), C. H. Dodd (*Moffatt*), Neil Alexander (*Torch*). There is a most helpful study of 1 John by Robert Law entitled *The Tests of Life*. It was first published in 1909, but remains in many ways the best general study of the letter.

21 · The conflict of ministries

The Second and Third Letters of John

'The old order changes' would be a good alternative title for these two letters. They are the shortest letters in the New Testament. One sheet of paper would hold each of them, and yet they deal with a situation of the greatest importance and of the most explosive possibilities, and it is a situation which consistently repeats itself throughout the history of the Church. These letters have got to do with strangers and with the practice of hospitality. In the ancient world hospitality was not so much a gracious extra as it was an absolute necessity and a Christian duty. Travel was difficult and dangerous, for robbers and brigands and pirates abounded, and apart from the great Roman military highways, roads were rough and primitive. The ancient Liturgy of St James in its intercessions remembers 'those at sea, on the roads and among strangers'. Inns were expensive, flea-ridden and filthy, and those who used them were far from respectable people, and the New Testament has frequent injunctions to hospitality. 'Practise hospitality,' Paul writes to the Romans (Romans 12: 13). 'Practise hospitality ungrudgingly to one another,' writes Peter (1 Peter 4: 9). In the Letter to the Romans Gaius is praised as being 'host to me and to the whole Church' (Romans 16: 23). The bishop must be a hospitable man (1 Timothy 3: 2; Titus 1: 8). But hospitality and the traveller brought their problems. And it is with these problems that these two letters deal.

132

There has been much discussion as to whom Second John was written. Second John is addressed to the elect lady (verse 1). Is the elect lady a person? If so, what was her name? Both the word for *elect* and the word for *lady* could be proper names. The letter could be written to the lady Electa, or to the elect Kyria. If the lady is a person, who was she? Some have thought that she could be Mary the mother of our Lord, since she was given into the care of John (John 19: 26, 27). *Kurios* is the Greek for *lord* or in the feminine, *kuria*, for *lady*. *Mar* is the Aramaic for lord or lady; and so it has been ingeniously suggested that the letter was written to Martha! On the whole both the language and the substance make it much more likely that the letter was written to a Church, just as Peter refers to the Church in Babylon in the same way (1 Peter 5: 13). So then let us turn to the substance of Second John.

The warning of Second John is against 'anyone who goes ahead and does not abide in the doctrine of Christ'. Any such person does not love God, and is not to be received. To receive him is to be identified with his wickedness, and it is to run the risk of losing their hard won faith (verses 7-11). The warning is against 'anyone who goes ahead'. That is to say, it is a warning against the progressives, against those who have gone out on new ways of thought and who have left the old behind.

The way of the progressive is always hard, whether it is in the right or the wrong direction that he is progressing. Social changes are resented. In the story of the Clogher Valley Railway in Ireland, it is told that when the first Sunday trains were run clergymen inveighed against those who used them and those who ran them. The railways were 'sending souls to the devil at the rate of sixpence a time'. 'Every sound of the railway whistle is answered by a shout in hell.' Still more, theological changes are resented, for there are those for whom theology is a static and not a dynamic thing. Heinz Zahrnt in his book *The*

Historical Jesus quotes some examples of this kind of thing from Germany. There are those who would want to lay it down: 'For us the text of the Bible which is binding on Church and theology and is therefore verbally inerrant is the German translation of Martin Luther in the text and canon as possessed by the Church . . . Anyone who ventures on the sacrilegious undertaking of revising the text places himself . . . *extra ecclesiam* (outside the Church).' 'Any exegesis which does not correspond with the articles of the Evangelical-Lutheran Church is *a priori* unsound.' This is as if to say that the only word of God is the Authorised Version and the only statement of the faith the Westminster Confession. If the riches of Christ are unsearchable and inexhaustible, then ever new truth must reward the search of the mind, and ever new wonder the love of the heart.

But there can be a progressiveness which progresses out of the Christian religion altogether. The point that John makes is that if our belief in Jesus Christ is right, then all other beliefs are right, and the essentials of belief in Jesus Christ are that we must believe that Jesus Christ came in the flesh and we must believe that Jesus Christ is the Son of God (2 John 7-9; cp. 1 John 4: 2, 15). And the essential of the Christian life is that we must love one another (2 John: 5). Christian thought must indeed progress, for God has always new discoveries for us to make, but, however far thought may adventure on new pathways, it can never leave behind the manhood of Jesus, the divinity of Jesus, and the brotherhood of man.

The situation in 3 John is even more interesting, and even more significant. John writes in praise of Gaius and of Demetrius (3 John: 1-4, 12). But he writes in strong condemnation of Diotrephes (3 John: 9, 10). And what is the fault of Diotrephes? He likes to put himself first, or, as we might put it, he likes to be master in his own house (3 John: 9). And in what way is this desire for the first place shown? It is shown in his rejection of certain visitors who have come to his congregation, and in his refusal to let anyone else receive them either (3 John: 10). By doing this Diotrephes challenges John's authority, an authority which John now tries to assert (3 John: 10), by rebuking Diotrephes and by insisting that the visitors must be welcomed and helped (3 John: 5-8).

What is the situation behind this domestic dispute? In the first days of the Church there were two kinds of ministry. There was a ministry which was not confirmed to one place, and whose writ ran throughout the whole Church, a ministry which had the whole Church as its sphere, and whose representatives travelled everywhere throughout the Church. This was the ministry of the apostles and the prophets. There was a ministry which was a local ministry, settled in one place, a ministry whose sphere was the congregation. This was the ministry of the elders and the deacons and the teachers.

It was not very long before the wandering, itinerant ministry became a problem. The first book of common order that the Church possessed was *The Teaching of the Twelve Apostles*, commonly known as *The Didache*, which is the Greek word for teaching and which dates to about A.D. 100. It lays it down that the wandering teacher is to be tested. If his teaching is perverted he is not to be received. If his teaching is 'for the increase of righteousness and knowledge of the Lord' he is to be received. One of the great problems was that there were men who managed to get themselves a soft living by moving from congregation to congregation and living on the Church's charity. *The Didache* lays down its tests. 'Let every Apostle who comes to you be received as the Lord, but let him not stay more than one day, or if need be a second as well; but if he stays three days, he is a false prophet. And when an apostle goes forth let him accept nothing but bread till he reaches his night's lodging; but if he asks for money, he is a false prophet. . . . And no prophet who orders a meal in a spirit shall eat of it; otherwise he is a false prophet. And every prophet who teaches the truth, if he does not do what he teaches, is a false prophet.' If a traveller comes, and wants to settle in a community, let him work at a trade, 'so that no man shall live in idleness because he is a Christian. But if he will not do so, he is making traffic of Christ; beware of such.' Clearly *The Didache* (chapters 11 and 12) shows the inbuilt danger of the itinerant ministry.

But there was a bigger problem than that, and it is the bigger problem which 3 John illustrates. In the beginning the itinerant ministry had all the prestige. Had these men not left home and work and family to be the wandering heralds of the Gospel? They were the elite of the Church. But the longer the Church went on, the stronger the local ministry became. The local ministry became the backbone of the Church. The congregation became the unit. Of course, there was still a very large and honourable place for the wandering ministry in the places in which the name of Jesus Christ had never been preached and in the missionary work of the Church. But in the local Churches the itinerant preachers became an anachronism. The local settled ministry resented them. They came to be regarded as trouble-makers and interferers. Their coming was often regarded as no better than a disturbance and a nuisance.

This is exactly the situation in 3 John. The itinerant preachers arrived in the congregations. Gaius was still sufficiently old-fashioned to welcome them, as was Demetrius. Diotrephes was a man of the new generation. To him the wandering preachers were an outworn institution, whose presence damaged rather than helped a congregation. In his congregation he would have nothing to do with them himself, and he barred the mfrom the homes of the members of his congregation, so far as he could.

Here is the clash between the old and the new, between the itinerant and the settled ministries.

And the trouble was that John too was becoming an anachronism. He is called the Elder in the first verse of both letters. The Elder does not in this case describe an ecclesiastical office, as it does with us now. Rather it means the aged one, the patriarch, the father of the Church. For many years John had been used to his word being law. What he had said was accepted. The preachers he had sent had been received. But now Diotrephes had challenged his authority. John still tried to exert that authority, and there were still some like Gaius and Demetrius who were prepared to bow before it. But the end was on the way. The day of the itinerant preacher was at an end, and the day of the local congregation had come.

It may be that John had come to that frame of mind which men who are old find it very hard to escape. 'Look to yourselves,' he says, 'that you may not lose what you have worked for' (2 John: 8). His tendency was to look back and to hold on to what had been achieved. The tendency of youth is to look forward and to think rather of the adventure of the future than the achievement of the past. It is when there are joined together in a perfect marriage the spirit which values the past and the spirit which hears the summons to new ways that the Church is at its strongest and its most effective.

Questions for discussion

1. Is the Church characteristically too attached to the old and too afraid of the new?

2. If we are to be truly and properly progressive, which Christian doctrines most need to be re-thought and re-stated?

3. What place is there for the itinerant evangelist in the present day Church? What place is there for campaigns and crusades carried out by travelling evangelists?

4. What ought we to do when we find a person or an institution exercising, or trying to exercise, a dominant influence in Church or in congregation for too long? Is it true that in the Church men tend to hang on to power for too long? When a minister retires from his congregation or from some other work in the Church, should he in some sense also retire from Presbytery and Assembly?

Further reading
Commentaries by William Barclay (*Daily Study Bible*), C. H. Dodd (*Moffatt*), J. P. Love (*Layman's Bible*), Greville P. Lewis (*Epworth Preacher's Commentaries*).

22 · Visions of the end

The Revelation of John

The last book in the Bible is notoriously the most difficult book in the Bible. It always has been. Away back in the fifth century Jerome said that the Revelation contains as many secrets as it does words. Another ancient scholar said that study of the Revelation either finds a man mad or makes him mad. Modern scholars have repeated this verdict. R. M. Grant says that the Revelation is the most enigmatic book in the New Testament. H. B. Swete recounts how Benson tells how he asked an intelligent reader: 'What is the form the book presents to you?' The answer was: 'It is chaos.' G. B. Caird in the most recent English commentary on the Revelation writes: 'Is not the untutored reader bound to end with the question: "What on earth is all this about?" '

This has had two results. In the first place F. V. Filson says that the Revelation seems to have aroused the most persistent protests when the New Testament was being built up. Of all books it had the greatest difficulty in establishing its place in the New Testament. Only three of the great New Testament manuscripts contain it in full. It was not even translated into Syriac until the late fifth century, and as late as the fourteenth century its place in the canon of the Syriac Church was not assured. There is no Greek commentary on it until the fifth or sixth century. It is the only New Testament book on which Calvin did not write a commentary.

Some years ago there came into the possession of the New Testament Department in Glasgow University James Denney's interleaved copy of the Greek New Testament. Denney had put his notes and his interpretations on the interleaving sheets; and of all the New Testament books only the Revelation was a complete blank.

Luther did not regard it as scripture at all. 'I hold it,' he said, 'to be neither apostolic nor prophetic . . . My spirit cannot acquiesce in the book. I abide by the books which present Christ pure and clear . . . After all, in it Christ is neither taught nor acknowledged.'

And so the second result of the difficulty of the Revelation is that there have been those who wished to banish it from the New Testament altogether. Zwingli, for instance, definitely rejected it. 'With the Apocalypse,' he says, 'we have no concern, for it is not a biblical book . . . The Apocalypse has no savour of the mouth or mind of John. I can, if I so will, reject its testimonies.'

There is a formidable opposition to the Revelation. And yet if the Revelation had gone missing from the New Testament something essential would have been lost. In the New Testament the Revelation is unique; there is no other book in the least like it. But the Revelation is a specimen of a kind of literature which was very common between the two Testaments and of which many examples still survive. It could even be said that the Revelation is a specimen of the kind of literature which was the most popular literary form of all between the Testaments.

These books were called *apocalypses*, and, as we know, the alternative title by which the Revelation is often known is The Apocalypse, in Greek *apokalupsis*. What were these apocalypses? Nothing would ever persuade the Jews that they were not the chosen people, and nothing would ever persuade them that some day this would be made apparent to the world. At first they looked forward to a Messiah of David's line, who would lead them to the glory and the triumph which was theirs by right. Bit by bit they began to see that they were so small a nation, and the world empires were so vast, that this triumph could not ever come about by human means and by natural historical processes. But this did not in the least destroy their faith. They came to believe that God himself would come striding into history and would personally intervene to make Israel what it ought to be.

So they worked out a time scheme. There was this present age which is wholly and irremediably bad, beyond cure and beyond reformation, fit only for utter destruction and annihilation. There was the age to come, in which there would be a new world of glory and of goodness and of plenty, an age in which at last the Jewish nation would enter into its proper place and destiny. But how was the one age to turn into the other? Not by any human means. The change would come on the Day of the Lord, when God entered directly into history and shattered the old world and created the new. It is the Day of the Lord that these apocalypses claim to describe. Some of the names of them are *The Book of Enoch, The Testament of the Twelve Patriarchs, The Sibylline Oracles, The Apocalypse of Baruch, Fourth Ezra.*

The characteristic of these apocalypses is that they are always very difficult to understand, because they are trying to describe the indescribable, and to present a picture of things that no eye has seen, that no ear has heard, and that have never entered into the mind of man. They are telling of the unutterable and unimaginable action of God when God enters the world in might. The difference between the prophet and the apocalyptist is that the prophet writes of the reformation of this world; the apocalyptist writes of what will happen when this world dissolves under the action of God.

But there is a regular pattern of events connected with the Day of the Lord. It would be a day of utter terror (Isaiah 13: 6-8); a day of cosmic disaster when the moon would turn to blood and the sun to darkness (Zephaniah 1: 14-15; Joel 2: 31); a time of utter disintegration, when blood would trickle from the wood, stones would speak, women would bear monsters, sweet water would become salt (4 Ezra 5: 4-9); a time of hatred when human relationships would be destroyed, when families would exterminate each other, when wars would decimate the world (Zechariah 14: 13, 14; 2 Baruch 48: 35-37; 70: 2-8); and finally a time of the devastating judgment of God (Isaiah 13: 9-11; 24: 21, 22; 66: 15, 16). This is what the Revelation is all about, and this is why it is so difficult a book.

There is something else at the back of the Revelation. The great characteristic of the Revelation is a blazing hatred of the Roman Empire. Paul had praised and supported the state (Romans 13: 1-7; 1 Timothy 2: 1, 2); Peter had bidden men to fear God and to honour the Emperor (1 Peter 2: 17). But for the John of the Revelation Rome is the great harlot, drunk with the blood of the saints and the martyrs (Revelation 17: 1-6). Why the difference?

Into the situation there had entered a new factor—Caesar worship. In the last days of the Republic and the early days of the Empire men in sheer gratitude had worshipped the spirit of Rome, which had brought peace and justice to the world. The spirit of Rome is incarnated in the Emperor and before long divine honours were being paid to the Emperor, especially in the East. At its widest the Roman Empire stretched from Britain to the Euphrates and from the Danube to North Africa. The great problem was to get one unifying principle. That principle was found in Caesar worship, much as the British

Commonwealth was united by a common loyalty to the crown.

Rome was not exclusive. But it did work out a system in which once a year a man burned a pinch of incense to the godhead of Caesar, and declared, 'Caesar is Lord'. Once he had done that, he could go and worship as he chose. This system had begun to bite towards the end of the first century. Nothing would make a Christian say, 'Caesar is Lord'. For him Jesus Christ alone was Lord. The Christian therefore seemed a disloyal citizen, and thus Christianity was under attack. Always at the back of the Revelation, especially in passages about the Beast, as in chapter 13, the background is the threat of the persecution consequent on Caesar worship, and that is why the clash between the Christian and the Roman Empire had come, and why Caesar worship is the Beast.

So, if we remember two things about Revelation, it will become less mysterious. It is an apocalypse, literally an unveiling, of the events which are to happen at the Day of the Lord, and part of the terror and trial of the end are due to the threat of Caesar worship which hung over the Church. If we remember that, it will make the Revelation easier to read, if we see that it falls into seven parts.

1. There is the Prologue which describes how John came to write the book (Revelation 1). It is to be noted that the John who wrote the Revelation is not the same John as the John who wrote the Gospel. The Greek of the two books is so different that the same person could hardly have written them.

2. Chapters 2 and 3 are the Letters to the Seven Churches, who must set their house in order before the last storm breaks.

3. Then in chapters 4 and 5 the scene shifts to heaven, and John has the vision of the very presence of God.

4. Then the book of destiny is opened (5: 1); and there comes what we might call a pre-view of the terrible events of the coming Day of the Lord, the birth pangs of the new age.

There is the opening of the seven seals, each bringing new disasters (6: 1-17). There are the seven trumpet blasts, each bringing new terror (8: 1-13; 9: 1-21; 11: 15-19). There are the seven bowls, each pouring out dreadful things (16: 1-21). Then there is war in heaven and the Devil is cast out and comes to earth (12); and the Beast comes and does his terrible work (13).

5. Then there comes the final defeat of the Beast (19: 19-21), followed by the thousand-year reign of the martyred saints (20: 1-6).

6. There follows the conflict to end all conflicts, after which the Devil is flung into the lake of fire, and there comes the general resurrection and the final judgment. (20: 7-15).

7. Finally, there is the picture of the new heaven and the new earth, and of the new Jerusalem (21: 1-22: 5).

Such is the pattern of the Revelation. Its aim is to tell of the terrible events of the Day of the Lord which will precede the new heaven and the new earth, and to strengthen men for the trials which should come. There is much that is obscure in the Revelation, but the one thing which it does say with absolute clarity is that in any time of trial God is with his people, and that in the end the victory is sure.

Questions for discussion

1. Do you think that it is really worthwhile wrestling with the difficulties of the Revelation, or would you agree with Luther and Zwingli that the Revelation is a book that the Christian might well leave alone?

2. Do you think that the idea of the two ages and of the Day of the Lord and of all its terrors have to be taken literally? If not, how are we going to restate them in a way that is relevant for today?

3. One of the problems of the Revelation is Millennarianism (Revelation 20: 1-6). This teaches that there will be a conflict

with the Devil and Satan; they will be conquered and temporarily confined to a pit for one thousand years. During that thousand years those who have died as martyrs will be raised and will live in happiness. Sometimes the happiness has been very materially pictured. The rest of the dead will sleep on until the final battle and the general resurrection. What do you think of Millennarianism? It is quite strong in some circles. Do you think it wise to erect a whole doctrine on no more than six verses of scripture? Ought the Church to make Millennarianism one of its essential doctrines?

4. In the time of the Revelation the Church and the State were in total conflict. Is there any danger of such a conflict today?

Further reading
Commentaries by William Barclay (*Daily Study Bible*), M. Kiddle (*Moffatt*), R. H. Preston and A. T. Hanson (*Torch*), G. B. Caird (*A. and C. Black*), T. S. Kepler. The surviving apocalyptic writings, which belong to the same class of literature as the Revelation, can be found in R. H. Charles *The Apocrypha and Pseudepigrapha of the Old Testament.*

CONCLUSION

Together we have made a journey through the New Testament from one end to the other; and when we come to the end we can only say: 'Here is richness. Here is infinite variety.' It has been said and said truly that there are as many ways to the stars as there are men to climb them. In the New Testament there are many ways to God. It was as a heretic that Jesus was condemned in his days upon earth; and there is a sense in which the New Testament is a vastly heretical book. Again and again we find it saying things which would horrify a strict and narrow orthodoxy. But in face of all this variety we are left with one question to ask and to try to answer. Is there in all the variety something basic? Amongst all the variations is there a dominant and unchanging theme? Is there a constant in the variety? Is there something which gives the diversity a unity? I think there is; I think that the New Testament is all the time saying three things.

1. The New Testament is saying that God is. To a modern man it seems strange that neither in the Old Testament nor in the New Testament does the Bible ever make any attempt to prove that God exists. For the New Testament God is an axiom. In geometry an axiom is a truth which itself is never proved, which does not need to be proved, but which is the basis of all other proofs. So, for the Bible the existence of God is that with which all else begins.

Basically, two things are said about God. First, God is the moving power behind all creation. This does not necessarily mean that God created the world in a week; but it does mean that God is the power which set all things going, whether creation happened in a week, or whether creation after billions of years is still going on.

The second thing that the New Testament says about God is that God did not only create the world; he is concerned for men; he cares for men, and not only for men, but for each individual man. God, said Augustine, loves each one of us as if there was only one of us to love.

Once I was involved in an argument and discussion with a man who is an atheist. He is no belligerent atheist without the gift of reverence; he is a man who has regretfully come to the conclusion that the world is perfectly explicable without God. But in this particular discussion he said that the idea that God cares for, is concerned for, loves, each individual person seemed to him the most magnificent conception to which the human mind had ever attained—and he wished with all his heart that he could believe it. The Christian does believe it. He believes that God is; that God is the power behind creation; and that God cares for every creature who is part of this creation.

2. The second basic thing which the New Testament says is that something has gone wrong with the relationship which ought to exist between man and God, and that it has gone wrong on man's side. Whatever that relationship ordinarily is, it is not what it was meant to be. Disobedience, distance, fear, at worst total disregard, at best wistful longing, have taken the place of the father-son relationship which should exist between man and God.

Herein lies the dilemma of God. No doubt God could have made man such that man automatically obeyed God; but without freedom of will there can be no such thing as goodness, for goodness must always depend on the freedom to make a free choice between two alternatives, between the higher and the lower, between saying yes and no to God. Man, as it has been said, is the only living creature who has it in his power deliberately to say no to God—and that is precisely what man has done. 'Our wills are ours to make them thine'—so it has been said—but for most men our wills are ours to keep them our own. The relationship between man and God has been a relationship of tension and resistance instead of a relationship of trust and obedience.

There is a break in the contact which should exist between man and God, and the breach is on man's side, not on God's.

3. The third thing which the New Testament says—and also the unique thing—is that Jesus came into this world to heal the breach between God and man, to restore the relationship.

To do this he must be at the same time fully and perfectly man, and fully and perfectly God. Thus, as the early fathers put it, he represents man to God, and God to man. The New Testament never forgets either side of the person of Jesus.

The New Testament has two main ways of looking at the way in which the work of Jesus was done.

(a) It looks at his work in terms of sacrifice. Since with the exception of Luke all the New Testament writers were Jews it could not be otherwise. It is always to be remembered that two things have to be said about sacrifice. First, according to Jewish thought sacrifice does not avail for sins 'of a high hand', for sins of proud and arrogant disobedience and defiance, for sins of callous and cold deliberation. It avails only for sins into which a man slipped unaware, or into which he was swept by some moment of impulse or tide of passion. Second, no sacrifice, the Jew believed, was of any avail in any case, unless it was accompanied by penitence, and by sorrow of heart. But apart from that, sacrifice was regarded as the means given and accepted by God to repair breaches in the covenant, the relationship, between Israel and himself.

That being so, it was inevitable that the early Jewish thinkers should think of the work of Jesus in terms of sacrifice. As they saw it, he was the perfect, the only sacrifice indeed without spot or blemish, the sacrifice to end all sacrifices; he was the lamb of God who takes away the sin of the world, the scape-goat who bears away the sins of the people.

(*b*) But there is another idea beside that. Sometimes the New Testament writers see Jesus as the demonstration of God, the human embodiment of what God is like in his attitude towards men. Jesus is the Word of God, the expression of the thought of God, the mind of God become a human person. And all through his earthly life, completed by his death on the Cross, Jesus is saying: 'God loves you like that. Nothing you can do can ever destroy the love of God.' And that demonstration of love is such that it cannot fail to stimulate an answering love in the heart of man.

But this view too involves sacrifice, for it cost the life and death of Jesus to demonstrate to men the love of God. The Church has never had an 'official' view of the Atonement, of the mechanics of the way in which God restores the relationship between man and God. It is left to a man to lay hold on that theory which satisfies his own heart.

So the New Testament has three great pillar truths—(1) God is, and God is the creator who is still intimately concerned for all his creatures; (2) In spite of that something has gone wrong with the relationship between man and God; man has used his free-will to take his own way rather than God's way; (3) Jesus is the person who puts the relationship right, either because he is the perfect sacrifice, or because his life and death are an irresistible demonstration of the love of God. The New Testament sets forth man's dilemma and God's remedy for it.